Our first Microwave Cookbook proved to be so popular we decided to give you a great variety of wonderful new recipes to add to your collection.
The microwave oven has become accepted as a brilliant addition to your kitchen appliances; however, many people use their oven only as a defrosting, reheating or instant coffee-making machine. Our new recipes in this book show the full potential of the oven and you have the choice of cooking complete meals or at least part of your meal using microwave energy.
The recipes are designed for cooks in a hurry and, of course, they are triple tested and every one is pictured.

Pamela Clark
FOOD EDITOR

ASSISTANT FOOD EDITOR: *Barbara Northwood*

DEPUTY EDITOR: *Enid Morrison*

CHIEF HOME ECONOMIST: *Jan Castorina*

HOME ECONOMISTS: *Jon Allen, Jane Ash, Wendy Berecry, Karen Green, Sue Hipwell, Louise Sakiris, Kathy Wharton*

STYLISTS: *Rosemary Ingram, Jacqui Hing, Carolyn Fienberg, Jennifer Wells*

PHOTOGRAPHERS: *Ashley Mackevicius, Paul Clarke, Andre Martin, Jon Macmichael, David Young*

EDITORIAL ASSISTANT: *Denise Prentice*

KITCHEN ASSISTANT: *Amy Wong*

PRODUCTION EDITOR: *Maryanne Blacker*

ART DIRECTOR: *David Collins*

SUB EDITOR: *Mary-Anne Danaher*

EDITORIAL ASSISTANT: *Louise McGeachie*

PUBLISHER: *Richard Walsh*

ASSOCIATE PUBLISHER: *Sally Milner*

Produced by The Australian Women's Weekly Home Library Division
Typeset by Photoset Computer Service Pty Ltd, Sydney, Australia
Printed by Dai Nippon Co Ltd, Tokyo, Japan
Published by Australian Consolidated Press, 54 Park Street, Sydney
Distributed by Network Distribution Company, 54 Park Street, Sydney

WE USED MICROWAVE OVENS FROM: National Panasonic; Sanyo Australia Pty Ltd; Sharp Corporation; Toshiba (Australia) Pty Ltd.

Microwave Cookbook 2.

Includes index.
ISBN 0 949892 85 8.

1. Microwave cookery. I. Title: Australian Women's Weekly.

641.5'882

BEFORE YOU START...

Open the door to understanding the magical microwave oven and how it can change your cooking style.

All our recipes have been triple tested in ovens which vary in output between 600 and 700 watts. The difference in the cooking times in these ovens is only about 10 percent, so we have given minimum approximate cooking times.

The golden rule for cooking successfully in all microwave ovens is to undercook, check the food, then cook with short bursts of microwave energy until the food is cooked as desired.

Variations in cooking times are due to many factors. These include the size, density and water content of the food, the size and shape of dish used, how the food is arranged in that dish, the age and capacity of the oven, and even where your house is in relation to the power supply.

These factors are not any different when applied to food cooked in a conventional way; it's just that the effects happen about three times faster in the microwave oven.

Since microwave cooking is so fast, most of the recipes have been designed for the cook in a hurry, so we suggest the recipes be made, then served immediately; there are many casseroles and dishes suitable for the organised cook to make and freeze for future use.

Food cooked in the microwave oven does not cook evenly because of the pattern of microwave energy distribution. Some ovens have stirrers or distributors which move the microwave energy around. Other ovens have turntables which rotate the food, so exposing it to the energy more evenly.

However, it is still necessary to stir food or rearrange the dishes during the cooking. Follow our instructions in individual recipes.

As a rule, if food needs to be turned, covered or stirred (or all three) when cooked conventionally, then it is also necessary in the microwave oven. Our recipes indicate when to turn, cover or stir; otherwise, presume it is not necessary.

Most of the recipes in this book serve four, which makes them easy to halve. However, due to size limitations of the oven, it is not advisable to make larger quantities than our recipes specify at the one time.

It is important you read the instruction manual that accompanies your oven.

Commonsense is the main requirement when using a microwave oven. They are safe, easy to use economical and time-saving. They heat the food, not the oven or kitchen, and cut down on dishes required for cooking – you will end up cooking lots of things in serving dishes!

COOKWARE

There is a great range of cookware designed for use in the microwave oven. However, you will find you can use most of the non-metal dishes you have in your kitchen.

If in doubt about the suitability of a dish or plate, etc, for use in a microwave oven, stand the dish in the oven with a glass of water next to it. Turn the control to HIGH, set for a minute. If the dish remains cold it is fine for use. If (like the water) it gets hot, don't use it in the microwave oven.

Many recipes in this book use a ring-shaped dish (see p66 for pictures and further information). The various dishes available are made from different materials, so be sure to read all accompanying literature to be certain the dish meets your requirements.

Foil food trays can be used if they are at least two-thirds full of food. Keep trays about 2cm away from walls and door of oven when closed.

BROWNING

Microwave ovens have long been accused of not browning any food. In fact, some foods brown quite well without any assistance; some need a mixture brushed over the surface; others benefit from browning on a special dish.

Steaks, chops, sausages, burgers, etc, will brown and seal well on a preheated browning dish. The addition of a little butter on the hot dish will help even more.

There are many different shapes and sizes of browning dishes specially designed for the microwave oven; these must not be used in a conventional oven.

These dishes seal and sear food well, provided the instructions are followed. It is important to preheat the dish to the time specified in the accompanying leaflet.

Place the food onto the surface, press food down with a spatula or egg slide, if possible, just as if you were barbecuing on a solid plate, then turn the food quickly to get maximum browning.

Naturally, the temperature of the food reduces the temperature of the surface, so preheat the dish again when necessary. Room temperature food will give best results.

The tiny feet under the browning dish stop direct contact with the turntable, preventing damage. Here are points to remember about browning dishes:

- Splattering is normal and a lid will reduce this, but will "steam" the food.
- The browning dish will be discoloured after use.
- Smoke in the oven is also normal.
- Always use oven mitts when handling these dishes as they become very hot.
- Never place a hot dish on an unprotected counter top.
- To clean dishes, use a cleaning agent recommended by the manufacturer.

COOKING TIPS

- We have deliberately left salt out of our recipes. It is wise to season lightly with any salt, herbs, sauce or flavouring after cooking or standing time, but this depends on the recipe.
- Pierce the membrane or skin of food with a skewer or fork before cooking, for example, egg yolks, potatoes and tomatoes.
- Don't deep or shallow fry in the microwave oven as the oil temperature cannot be controlled.

APPETISERS

Serve these tempting savouries with drinks before dinner. They are all deliciously simple to make and most can be prepared ahead of cooking time.

PORK AND VEAL WONTONS

Wontons can be prepared for cooking up to a day ahead; uncooked wontons can be frozen for up to a month and thawed in refrigerator overnight before they are required.

30g butter
2 green shallots, chopped
1 clove garlic, crushed
2 teaspoons plain flour
125g pork and veal mince
125g mushrooms, finely chopped
2 teaspoons oyster sauce
½ teaspoon sesame oil
18 wonton wrappers
1 teaspoon cornflour
1 tablespoon water
DIPPING SAUCE
2 tablespoons hoisin sauce
1 tablespoon dark soya sauce

Combine butter, shallots and garlic in a dish. Cook on HIGH for 2 minutes, stir in flour, mince, mushrooms, oyster sauce and sesame oil.

Place a heaped teaspoon of mushroom mixture in the centre of each wonton wrapper. Brush edge of pastry with a little of the blended cornflour and water. Pinch opposite corners of pastry together.

Pour enough hot water into a shallow dish to come 2cm up side of dish, cover, cook on HIGH for about 5 minutes or until water is boiling. Place wontons in the water, cover, cook on HIGH for about 5 minutes or until wontons are cooked through. Serve with dipping sauce.

Dipping Sauce: Combine ingredients.

Makes 18.

SEAFOOD LETTUCE ROLLS

Rolls can be prepared up to a day ahead. Recipe unsuitable to freeze.

15 lettuce leaves
30 fresh chives
250g white fish fillets
125g scallops
1 egg
½ cup stale breadcrumbs
1 teaspoon lemon juice
¼ cup chopped fresh chives, extra
DIPPING SAUCE
¼ cup light soya sauce
2 tablespoons hoisin sauce

Place lettuce leaves in a large shallow dish, cover, cook on HIGH for about 4 minutes or until just wilted, drain on absorbent paper. Place chives in shallow dish, cover, cook on HIGH for about 30 seconds or until bright green.

Blend or process boned fish and scallops until smooth, add egg, breadcrumbs, lemon juice and extra chives, process until smooth.

Cut each lettuce leaf in half, place a teaspoonful of fish mixture on each half, fold in sides and roll up. Tie each roll with a chive, place in a shallow dish, cook on HIGH for about 4 minutes or until rolls are cooked through. Serve with dipping sauce.

Dipping Sauce: Combine ingredients.

Makes 30.

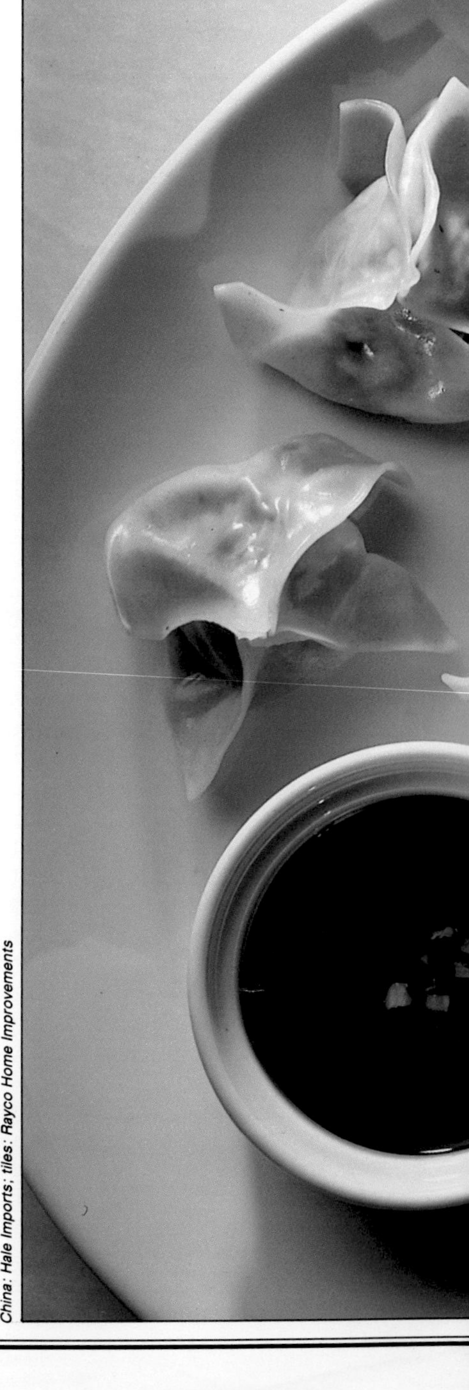

Left: Pork and Veal Wontons; right: Seafood Lettuce Rolls.

China: Hale Imports; tiles: Rayco Home Improvements

BACON AND MUSHROOM VOL-AU-VENTS

Vol-au-vent cases can be filled several hours ahead and heated just before serving. Recipe unsuitable to freeze.

15g butter
2 green shallots, finely chopped
2 bacon rashers, finely chopped
100g mushrooms, finely chopped
1 tablespoon plain flour
½ cup milk
¼ cup grated tasty cheese
2 tablespoons packaged breadcrumbs
1 tablespoon chopped fresh parsley
36 small vol-au-vent cases

Combine butter, shallots and bacon in a bowl, cover, cook on HIGH for 2 minutes, stir in mushrooms, cover, cook on HIGH for 2 minutes. Stir in flour, cook on HIGH for 1 minute. Stir in milk, cook on HIGH for about 2 minutes or until mixture boils and thickens, stir in the cheese.

Place teaspoonfuls of mixture into vol-au-vent cases, sprinkle with combined breadcrumbs and parsley.

Cover a plate with absorbent paper, place one-third of the filled vol-au-vents on the plate, cook on HIGH for 1 minute, transfer to serving plate.

Repeat in the same way with remaining vol-au-vents.

Makes 36.

CHICKEN LIVERS AND BACON ON PUMPERNICKEL

Chicken liver mixture can be frozen for up to 2 months.

30g butter
1 clove garlic, crushed
1 medium onion, chopped
2 bacon rashers, chopped
250g chicken livers, finely chopped
1 canned pimiento, drained, chopped
1 tablespoon chopped fresh oregano
250g packet pumpernickel rounds

Combine butter, garlic, onion and bacon in a shallow dish, cover, cook on HIGH for 3 minutes. Stir in livers, pimiento and oregano, cover, cook on HIGH for about 4 minutes or until livers are tender. Top each pumpernickel round with a teaspoon of mixture.

Makes about 25.

China: Incorporated Agencies; tiles: Rayco Home Improvements

Left: Mini Tostadas; Right: From top: Chicken Livers and Bacon on Pumpernickel; Zucchini Slices; Cheesy Mince Balls in Bacon Wraps; Bacon and Mushroom Vol-au-Vents.

MINI TOSTADAS

Taco sauce is available in most supermarkets. Recipe unsuitable to freeze.

100g packet corn chips
130g can baked beans
¼ cup taco sauce
1 cup grated tasty cheese

Line a large, shallow dish with absorbent paper. Place chips in a single layer in dish. Top chips with a few beans, a little sauce, then cheese. Cook on HIGH for about 1 minute.

Makes about 60.

CHEESY MINCE BALLS IN BACON WRAPS

Mince balls can be prepared for cooking up to 2 days ahead or frozen for up to 2 months; thaw in refrigerator.

250g minced beef
2 teaspoons French mustard
2 green shallots, chopped
2 tablespoons grated tasty cheese
1 tablespoon stale breadcrumbs
3 bacon rashers

Combine beef, mustard, shallots, cheese and breadcrumbs in a bowl, mix well. Shape tablespoons of mixture into balls, wrap in a thin strip of bacon, secure with a toothpick. Place in a single layer in a large, shallow dish, cook on HIGH for about 3 minutes or until mince balls are cooked through.

Makes about 20.

ZUCCHINI SLICES

Recipe unsuitable to freeze.

4 medium zucchini
1 tablespoon water
RICOTTA TOPPING
90g ricotta cheese
1 teaspoon grated parmesan cheese
1 tablespoon chopped fresh chives
1 teaspoon chopped fresh basil
BREADCRUMB TOPPING
1 tablespoon stale breadcrumbs
1 tablespoon grated parmesan cheese
paprika

Cut zucchini into 2cm rounds. Place in a shallow dish in a single layer, add the water, cover, cook on HIGH for 1 minute. Remove from dish and rinse in cold water; drain.

Scoop a little flesh out of each zucchini slice, spread with ricotta mixture, sprinkle with breadcrumb mixture and paprika. Cook on HIGH for about 30 seconds or until hot.

Ricotta Topping: Combine cheeses and herbs in a small bowl; mix well.
Breadcrumb Topping: Combine breadcrumbs and cheese in a bowl.

Makes about 24.

SOUPS

Most of our soups need blending or processing; blending will give a finer texture but mixtures can be pushed through a sieve, if preferred. We have not suggested reheating times as these will vary according to the temperature of the soup and the amount you plan to reheat. It is often easier to reheat soup in individual serving dishes instead of in large amounts.

SEAFOOD BISQUE

We used snapper cutlets in this recipe.

30g butter
1 clove garlic, crushed
1 medium onion, chopped
1 medium sweet potato, chopped
1 small fresh red chilli, chopped
2 small chicken stock cubes, crumbled
2 cups hot water
425g can tomatoes
1 bay leaf
2 tablespoons tomato paste
500g white fish cutlets

Left: Carrot and Stilton Soup; right: Seafood Bisque.

Soup bowls: Incorporated Agencies; tiles: Pazotti

375g uncooked prawns, shelled
¼ cup cream

Combine butter, garlic and onion in a large bowl, cover, cook on HIGH for 3 minutes. Add potato and chilli, cover, cook on HIGH for 5 minutes. Stir in stock cubes, water, undrained crushed tomatoes, bay leaf and tomato paste, cover, cook on HIGH for 4 minutes. Remove bay leaf. Blend or process mixture in several batches until smooth; return to bowl.

Remove skin and bones from fish, cut fish into 2cm pieces. Add fish and prawns to tomato mixture, cover, cook on HIGH for about 3 minutes or until prawns turn pink. Add cream, reheat without boiling.

Serves 4.

CARROT AND STILTON SOUP

If stilton cheese is not available, use a blue cheese instead. Recipe unsuitable to freeze.

60g butter
3 medium carrots, chopped
1 small chicken stock cube, crumbled
2 cups hot water
60g stilton cheese, crumbled
½ cup cream

Combine butter and carrots in a large bowl, cover, cook on HIGH for about 6 minutes or until carrots are tender. Add stock cube and water, cover, cook on HIGH for 6 minutes. Blend or process mixture in several batches until smooth; return to bowl. Add cheese and cream, reheat without boiling. Serve sprinkled with a little extra cheese, if preferred.

Serves 4.

CURRIED CHICKEN AND ASPARAGUS SOUP

Recipe unsuitable to freeze.

2 chicken breast fillets
1 cup hot water
1 chicken stock cube, crumbled
30g butter
1 medium onion, chopped
2 tablespoons plain flour
2 teaspoons curry powder
½ teaspoon ground cumin
1½ cups milk
440g can asparagus cuts, drained

Combine chicken, water and stock cube in a large bowl, cover, cook on HIGH for about 4 minutes or until chicken is just tender. Drain chicken, reserve stock.

Combine butter and onion in a large bowl, cover, cook on HIGH for 3 minutes, stir in flour, curry powder and cumin, cook on HIGH for 1 minute. Stir in reserved stock and milk, cook on HIGH for about 3 minutes or until soup boils and thickens, stir occasionally. Stir in chopped chicken and asparagus, cook on HIGH for about 1 minute or until heated through.

Serves 4.

PIMIENTO TOMATO SOUP

Soup can be frozen for a month.

60g butter
6 green shallots, chopped
2 bacon rashers, chopped
3 canned pimientos, drained, chopped
2 x 425g cans tomatoes
1 small chicken stock cube, crumbled
1½ cups water
1 tablespoon chopped fresh thyme
1 tablespoon sugar
2 tablespoons sour cream

Combine butter, shallots, bacon and pimiento in a large bowl, cover, cook on HIGH for 3 minutes. Add undrained crushed tomatoes, stock cube, water, thyme and sugar, cover, cook on HIGH for 5 minutes.

Blend or process mixture in several batches until smooth. Reheat before serving, top with sour cream.

Serves 4.

Top: Curried Chicken and Asparagus Soup; bottom: Pimiento Tomato Soup.

Soup bowls: Hale Imports; tiles: Pazotti

Soup bowls: Pillivuyt; tiles: Pazotti

Clockwise from left: Hearty Corn Chowder; Chilli Lentil Soup; Coriander and Ham Soup.

CHILLI LENTIL SOUP

Soup can be prepared up to 3 days ahead or frozen for up to 2 months.

1 cup red lentils
30g butter
1 medium onion, chopped
1 teaspoon grated fresh ginger
1 clove garlic, crushed
1 small fresh red chilli, chopped
½ teaspoon ground cardamom
½ teaspoon turmeric
2 small chicken stock cubes, crumbled
2¼ cups hot water
½ cup coconut cream
1 teaspoon chopped fresh coriander

Soak lentils in hot water for 10 minutes; drain. Combine butter, onion, ginger, garlic, chilli and spices in a large bowl, cover, cook on HIGH for 3 minutes. Add lentils, stock cubes and water, cover, cook on HIGH for about 10 minutes or until lentils are tender, stir several times during cooking. Blend or process mixture in several batches until smooth, add coconut cream and coriander, process until combined. Reheat before serving.

Serves 4.

HEARTY CORN CHOWDER

Recipe unsuitable to freeze.

3 bacon rashers, chopped
1 medium onion, finely chopped
1½ tablespoons plain flour
2½ cups milk
1 egg, lightly beaten
½ teaspoon paprika
310g can creamed corn
300g can corn kernels, drained
1 tablespoon chopped fresh parsley
½ cup sour cream

Combine bacon and onion in a large bowl. Cover, cook on HIGH for 3 minutes. Blend flour with ¼ cup of the milk, stir into bacon mixture, cook on HIGH for about 5 minutes or until mixture is thick and bubbly. Stir in remaining milk, egg, paprika, corn and parsley. Cook on HIGH for about 8 minutes; stir several times during cooking. Stir in cream; reheat before serving.

Serves 4.

CORIANDER AND HAM SOUP

Recipe unsuitable to freeze.

30g butter
1 medium onion, chopped
1 clove garlic, crushed
100g ham, chopped
½ cup lightly packed fresh coriander leaves
¼ cup fresh parsley sprigs
3 cups hot water
2 small chicken stock cubes, crumbled

Combine butter, onion, garlic and ham in a large bowl, cover, cook on HIGH for 3 minutes. Add coriander, parsley, water and stock cubes, cover, cook on HIGH for 12 minutes. Blend or process in several batches until smooth; reheat before serving.

Serves 4.

LEEK AND CORN SOUP

Recipe can be made up to 2 days ahead; store, covered, in refrigerator. Soup can be frozen for 2 months.

2 medium leeks, thinly sliced
60g butter
1 tablespoon plain flour
3 cups hot water
2 small chicken stock cubes, crumbled
440g can creamed corn
2 tablespoons sour cream

Combine leeks and butter in a large bowl, cover, cook on HIGH for 5 minutes. Add flour, stir until smooth. Stir in water, stock cubes and corn, cover, cook on HIGH for 5 minutes. Blend or process mixture in several batches until smooth.

Reheat before serving, top with sour cream.

Serves 4.

CAULIFLOWER AND LEEK SOUP

Recipe unsuitable to freeze.

½ small cauliflower
30g butter
1 medium leek, thinly sliced
2½ cups milk
2 tablespoons grated parmesan cheese
2 tablespoons chopped fresh parsley

Cut cauliflower into flowerets, rinse well under cold water; do not dry. Place cauliflower in a single layer in a dish, cover, cook on HIGH for about 8 minutes or until tender; drain.

Combine butter and leek in a small bowl, cook on HIGH for about 5 minutes or until leek is tender. Blend cauliflower, leek mixture and milk in several batches until smooth, transfer to large bowl. Stir in cheese and parsley, cook on HIGH for about 4 minutes or until heated through.

Serves 4.

Soup bowl: Incorporated Agencies

PASTA, ZUCCHINI AND TOMATO SOUP

Soup is best made then served immediately as it will thicken on standing. Recipe unsuitable to freeze.

30g butter
1 medium onion, chopped
1 clove garlic, crushed
440g can tomato purée
2 cups hot water
1 small chicken stock cube, crumbled
80g (1 cup) pasta
1 medium zucchini, sliced
1 tablespoon grated parmesan cheese
1 tablespoon chopped fresh parsley

Combine butter, onion and garlic in a large bowl, cover, cook on HIGH for 3 minutes. Add tomato purée, water and stock cube, cover, cook on HIGH for 10 minutes. Add pasta, cover, cook on HIGH for 4 minutes, stir in zucchini, cover, cook on HIGH for about 6 minutes or until pasta is soft. Stir in cheese and parsley.

Serves 4.

PUMPKIN PARMESAN SOUP

Soup can be made 2 days in advance and can be frozen for 2 months. Add cream and cheese when reheating.

500g pumpkin, chopped
30g butter
1 medium onion, chopped
1 clove garlic, crushed
3 cups hot water
2 small chicken stock cubes, crumbled
1 tablespoon tomato paste
¼ cup cream
1 tablespoon grated parmesan cheese

Combine pumpkin, butter, onion and garlic in a large bowl, cover, cook on HIGH for 7 minutes. Add water, stock cubes and tomato paste, cover, cook on HIGH for about 15 minutes or until pumpkin is tender. Blend or process in several batches until smooth; reheat, stir in cream, sprinkle with cheese.

Serves 4.

LEFT: Leek and Corn Soup.
RIGHT: Clockwise from left: Cauliflower and Leek Soup; Pumpkin Parmesan Soup; Pasta, Zucchini and Tomato Soup.

Soup bowls: Opus; tiles: Pazotti

SNACKS

Our snacks are super-tasty mini meals, quick to prepare and great to give to hungry kids after school or on occasions when friends or the sports crowd drop in. All recipes can be prepared with minimum fuss.

MUSHROOM AND HAM POCKETS

Recipe unsuitable to freeze.

2 small pita breads
1½ cups grated tasty cheese
75g mushrooms, sliced
100g ham, chopped
2 tablespoons tomato paste
2 tablespoons chopped fresh parsley

Cut each bread in half, gently open each half to form a pocket. Combine remaining ingredients in bowl, mix well; spoon mixture into pockets. Place pockets on a flat dish covered with absorbent paper. Cook on HIGH for about 2 minutes or until heated through.

Makes 4.

CORN AND SALAMI MUFFINS

Recipe unsuitable to freeze.

15g butter
1 small onion, finely chopped
310g can creamed corn
4 slices (40g) salami, chopped
¼ cup grated tasty cheese
1 tablespoon chopped fresh parsley
4 muffins
paprika

Combine butter and onion in a small bowl, cover, cook on HIGH for 3 minutes. Add corn and salami, cook on HIGH for about 1 minute or until heated through. Stir in cheese and parsley, cook on HIGH for 1 minute. Split muffins in half, toast, top with corn mixture, sprinkle with paprika.

Serves 4.

CRUNCHY SALAMI STICKS

Recipe unsuitable to freeze.

6 twin bread rolls
15g butter
1 tablespoon pine nuts
1 clove garlic, crushed
100g salami, chopped
¼ cup grated mozzarella cheese
2 tablespoons chopped fresh basil
2 tablespoons grated parmesan cheese

Split each roll into 2 pieces; halve rolls lengthways. Remove soft centre from each half, blend or process centres until finely crumbed.

Combine butter, pine nuts and garlic in bowl, cook on HIGH for 1 minute. Stir in salami, mozzarella cheese, basil and breadcrumbs, spoon mixture into bread roll shells, sprinkle with parmesan cheese.

Cover a flat dish with absorbent paper, cook half the salami sticks on HIGH for 1½ minutes. Repeat with remaining salami sticks.

Makes 24.

Clockwise from top: Mushroom and Ham Pockets; Crunchy Salami Sticks; Corn and Salami Muffins.

Plates: Villa Italiana

CHEESY HAM CROISSANTS

Recipe unsuitable to freeze.

1½ cups grated tasty cheese
100g ham, chopped
1 medium tomato, chopped
¼ cup sour cream
1 tablespoon mayonnaise
2 teaspoons French mustard
4 croissants

Combine cheese, ham, tomato, cream, mayonnaise and mustard in a bowl. Slit back of each croissant, fill with ham mixture, place on a flat dish covered with absorbent paper. Cook on HIGH for about 2 minutes or until hot.

Makes 4.

SPICY MEATBALLS WITH TANGY CHEESE DIP

Uncooked meatballs can be frozen for up to 2 months. Chevre is an imported cheese available from most delicatessens and gourmet stores; if not available, a soft creamy blue vein cheese could be substituted.

125g minced beef
125g sausage mince
2 green shallots, chopped
1 tablespoon tomato sauce
½ teaspoon ground coriander
½ teaspoon curry powder
¼ teaspoon chilli powder
¼ teaspoon paprika

CHEESE DIP
60g chevre cheese, chopped
60g tasty cheese, chopped
2 tablespoons milk
1 tablespoon chopped fresh parsley
½ teaspoon Worcestershire sauce

Combine minces, shallots, tomato sauce and spices in a bowl. Roll teaspoonfuls of mixture into balls, place in a shallow dish in a single layer, cook on HIGH for 4 minutes.

Drain excess liquid from dish, cook further 2 minutes or until meat balls are cooked through. Cover with foil while preparing cheese dip.

Cheese Dip: Combine all ingredients in a shallow dish, cook on HIGH for about 1 minute or until cheese is melted, stir occasionally.

Makes about 16.

SAVOURY PITA WEDGES

Recipe unsuitable to freeze.

60g butter
1 teaspoon dried oregano leaves
1 tablespoon seeded mustard
2 small pita breads
¼ cup grated parmesan cheese
½ teaspoon paprika
¼ cup stuffed olives, chopped

Combine butter and oregano in a small bowl, cover, cook on HIGH for 1 minute; stir in mustard. Cut each bread into 8 wedges, split wedges open without cutting through. Brush inside wedges with butter mixture, place wedges on a flat dish covered with absorbent paper. Sprinkle with cheese and paprika, top with olives, cook on HIGH for about 2 minutes or until heated through.

Makes 16.

Plate: Accoutrement

LEFT: Spicy Meatballs with Tangy Cheese Dip; ABOVE: Savoury Pita Wedges; BELOW: Cheesy Ham Croissants.

China: Villeroy & Boch

POTATO BACON YUMS

Recipe unsuitable to freeze.

10 small new potatoes
¼ cup chopped fresh parsley
60g fetta cheese, crumbled
2 bacon rashers, finely chopped

Place potatoes in a large bowl with hot water, cover, cook on HIGH for about 10 minutes or until potatoes are tender; drain. Cut top from each potato, carefully scoop out potato pulp, do not break outside skin of potato.

Combine parsley, cheese, bacon and potato pulp. Spoon back into potato shells, place on flat dish, cover, cook on HIGH for about 2 minutes or until heated through.

Makes 10.

BACON-WRAPPED SAUSAGES WITH SPICY SAUCE

This recipe can be prepared for cooking up to a day ahead; prepared sausages are unsuitable to freeze.

½ cup tomato sauce
2 tablespoons Worcestershire sauce
2 tablespoons brown sugar
1 tablespoon brown vinegar
¼ teaspoon chilli powder
2 teaspoons cornflour
¼ cup water
4 bacon rashers
500g baby sausages (chipolatas)

Combine sauces, sugar, vinegar, chilli and blended cornflour and water in a bowl, cook on HIGH for about 3 minutes or until sauce boils and thickens; stir occasionally.

Cut bacon into 6cm strips. Wrap bacon around each sausage, secure with toothpicks. Brush sausages with sauce mixture, place half the sausages around the edge of a shallow dish, cook on HIGH for about 4 minutes or until sausages are cooked. Repeat with remaining sausages. Reheat remaining sauce in bowl on HIGH for about 1 minute. Serve with sauce.

Serves 4.

Plate: Incorporated Agencies

Table: Freedom Furniture

MINI HOT DOGS WITH MUSTARD BUTTER

Recipe unsuitable to freeze.

60g soft butter
⅔ cup grated mozzarella cheese
2 teaspoons prepared mustard
1 tablespoon chopped fresh parsley
3 twin bread rolls
12 cocktail frankfurts

Combine butter, cheese, mustard and parsley in a bowl; mix well. Break each roll into 2 pieces. Cut each piece in half crossways. Split each piece lengthways on one side only. Spread rolls evenly with butter mixture.

Place a frankfurt in centre of each piece of roll. Place mini hot dogs on a flat dish covered with absorbent paper, cover with more absorbent paper, cook on HIGH for about 2 minutes or until they are heated through. Serve with tomato sauce, if desired.

Makes 12.

SALMON, MUSHROOM AND BACON ROLLS

Recipe unsuitable to freeze.

4 bread rolls
2 bacon rashers, chopped
60g mushrooms, chopped
105g can salmon, drained
1 cup grated tasty cheese
1 tablespoon chopped fresh parsley

Cut top from each roll, reserve tops; hollow out rolls. Sprinkle bacon over absorbent paper, place on flat dish, top with more absorbent paper, cook on HIGH for about 1 minute or until crisp.

Combine bacon, mushrooms, flaked salmon, cheese and parsley in a bowl, mix well, spoon mixture into rolls, replace tops. Place on flat dish, cook on HIGH for about 2 minutes or until heated through.

Makes 4.

Table: Freedom Furniture

LEFT: Top: Bacon-Wrapped Sausages with Spicy Sauce; right: Potato Bacon Yums; FAR LEFT: Mini Hot Dogs with Mustard Butter; ABOVE: Salmon, Mushroom and Bacon Rolls.

SEAFOOD

Seafood is wonderfully quick, easy and tasty when cooked in the microwave oven, and you will always have perfect results if you remember these three points: try to choose uniformly sized pieces of seafood, turn or stir the food for even cooking and most importantly, avoid overcooking.

China: Limoges; background laminate: Abet Laminati

China & cutlery: Limoges; tiles: Country Floors

HONEY GLAZED PRAWNS

Recipe unsuitable to freeze.

1kg uncooked king prawns, shelled
⅓ cup honey
2 tablespoons light soya sauce
2 tablespoons hoisin sauce
2 tablespoons dry sherry
1 clove garlic, crushed
2 teaspoons grated fresh ginger
2 tablespoons oil

Devein prawns, leaving tails intact. Combine honey, sauces, sherry, garlic and ginger in a large shallow dish, add prawns, mix well, cover, refrigerate several hours or overnight.

Heat a browning dish, place oil on dish, add drained prawns in a single layer, turn to quickly seal other side, then cook on HIGH for 3 minutes, turning once during cooking.

Serves 4.

FISH ROLLS WITH CREAMY DILL MAYONNAISE

We used whiting fillets in this recipe; it is unsuitable to freeze.

8 uncooked king prawns, shelled
⅓ cup packaged breadcrumbs
2 tablespoons chopped fresh parsley
1 tablespoon lemon juice
8 small white fish fillets
¼ cup dry white wine
¼ cup lemon juice, extra
30g butter

CREAMY DILL MAYONNAISE

⅔ cup mayonnaise
⅓ cup thickened cream
2 teaspoons lemon juice
1 teaspoon chopped fresh dill

Devein prawns, combine breadcrumbs, parsley and lemon juice; spread mixture evenly over one side of each fish fillet. Top each fillet with a prawn, roll up, secure with toothpicks. Place the fish rolls in a single layer in a large shallow dish, add combined wine and extra lemon juice, dot with butter, cover, cook on HIGH for about 8 minutes or until fish is tender. Remove toothpicks. Serve hot fish with cold mayonnaise.

Creamy Dill Mayonnaise: Combine all ingredients in a small bowl.

Serves 4.

LEFT: Clockwise from top: Fish with Prawn and White Wine Sauce; Fish in Tamarind Sauce; Fish Rolls with Creamy Dill Mayonnaise. FAR LEFT: Honey Glazed Prawns.

FISH IN TAMARIND SAUCE

We used bream fillets in this recipe; it is unsuitable to freeze.

4 white fish fillets
¼ cup tamarind sauce
2 tablespoons water
¼ teaspoon ground cumin
1 teaspoon grated fresh ginger
2 teaspoons sugar
3 green shallots, chopped
1½ teaspoons cornflour
1 tablespoon water, extra

Place fish in a single layer in a large shallow dish, cover, cook on HIGH for about 4 minutes or until fish is tender.

Combine tamarind sauce, water, cumin, ginger, sugar and shallots in a small bowl, cover, cook on HIGH for 1 minute. Stir blended cornflour and extra water into tamarind mixture, cook on HIGH for about 1 minute or until sauce boils and thickens. Pour sauce over fish just before serving.

Serves 4.

FISH WITH PRAWN AND WHITE WINE SAUCE

We used ocean perch fillets in this recipe; it is unsuitable to freeze.

4 thick white fish fillets
2 teaspoons lemon juice
PRAWN AND WHITE WINE SAUCE
¾ cup water
¼ cup dry white wine
1 stick celery, chopped
1 medium onion, chopped
1 bay leaf
60g butter
1½ tablespoons plain flour
1 egg yolk
250g uncooked king prawns, shelled, chopped
1 tablespoon lemon juice

Place fish in a single layer in a large shallow dish, sprinkle fish with lemon juice, cover, cook on HIGH for 4 minutes. Serve with sauce.

Prawn and White Wine Sauce: Combine water, wine, celery, onion and bay leaf in a bowl, cover, cook on HIGH for 3 minutes. Strain, reserve liquid. Melt butter in a bowl on HIGH for 1 minute, stir in flour, then reserved liquid and egg yolk, cook on HIGH for about 3 minutes or until mixture boils and thickens; stir occasionally. Stir in prawns and juice, cook on HIGH for about 1 minute or until tender.

Serves 4.

China: Limoges

SQUID WITH CORN AND DILL

Recipe unsuitable to freeze.

500g squid hoods
1 tablespoon lime juice
1 bunch fresh asparagus
1 tablespoon water
1 tablespoon oil
1 clove garlic, crushed
425g can whole baby corn, drained
1 tablespoon dry sherry
⅓ cup tomato purée
1 tablespoon chopped fresh dill

Cut squid into rings, place in a bowl with lime juice, stand 30 minutes.

Place asparagus in a large shallow dish with the water, cover, cook on HIGH for 1 minute, drain, cut in half.

Heat oil in a large shallow dish, add garlic, squid and corn, cover, cook on HIGH for 2 minutes. Add sherry, tomato purée and asparagus, cover, cook on HIGH for about 2 minutes or until squid is tender; stir occasionally. Sprinkle with dill.

Serves 4.

CHUNKY FISH WITH MUSTARD HONEY SAUCE

We used boneless, skinless gemfish in this recipe; it is unsuitable to freeze.

750g white fish fillets
15g butter
2 tablespoons dry white wine
2 teaspoons seeded mustard
½ teaspoon French mustard
2 teaspoons honey
60g butter, extra
½ teaspoon cornflour
1 teaspoon water
3 green shallots, chopped

Cut fish into bite-sized pieces. Melt butter in a large shallow dish on HIGH for 15 seconds, add fish, cover, cook on HIGH for about 4 minutes or until fish is just tender; stir occasionally during cooking; drain.

Combine wine, mustards and honey in a small bowl, cook on HIGH for 1 minute, whisk in extra butter a little at a time. Blend cornflour with water, stir into mustard mixture with shallots, cook on HIGH for about 1 minute or until sauce boils and thickens; stir halfway through the cooking time. Serve sauce over fish.

Serves 4.

CREAMY SEAFOOD AND POTATO CASSEROLE

We used ling fish fillets in this recipe; it is unsuitable to freeze.

500g white fish fillets
375g cooked prawns, shelled
500g new potatoes, chopped
¼ cup water
60g butter
1 medium red pepper, chopped
1 medium onion, sliced
½ cup dry white wine
½ cup cream
¼ cup sour cream
1 egg yolk

Cut fish into bite-sized pieces. Devein prawns, leaving tails intact. Place potatoes in single layer in a shallow dish with the water, cover, cook on HIGH for about 8 minutes or until potatoes are tender. Drain potatoes, rinse under cold water, drain. Combine butter, pepper and onion in a large shallow dish, cover, cook on HIGH for 3 minutes. Stir in fish, potatoes, wine, cream and sour cream, cover, cook on HIGH for about 4 minutes or until fish is tender. Stir in egg yolk and prawns, cook on HIGH, without boiling, for about 1 minute or until hot.

Serves 4.

Dish: Pillivuyt from The Bay Tree; tiles: Pazotti

ABOVE: From left: Squid with Corn and Dill; Chunky Fish with Mustard Honey Sauce; Hot 'n' Spicy Sole. LEFT: Creamy Seafood and Potato Casserole.

HOT 'N' SPICY SOLE

Recipe unsuitable to freeze.

2 medium sole
½ teaspoon ground coriander
½ teaspoon ground cumin
1 clove garlic, crushed
1 teaspoon curry powder
2 teaspoons oil
2 teaspoons lime juice
¼ teaspoon sambal oelek
2 teaspoons fruit chutney
30g butter

Remove skin from sole, slash with a sharp knife at 2cm intervals over both sides of fish. Combine remaining ingredients except butter in a small bowl, rub all over the fish, stand 1 hour. Melt butter in a large shallow dish on HIGH for 30 seconds. Add fish, brush with butter. Cook on HIGH for about 2 minutes or until sole is tender.

Serves 2.

HERBED OCTOPUSES IN RED WINE SAUCE

Recipe unsuitable to freeze.

1kg baby octopuses
30g butter
3 green shallots, chopped
1 tablespoon chopped fresh oregano
1 tablespoon sugar
¼ cup dry red wine
425g can tomatoes
2 tablespoons tomato paste

Clean octopuses, discard heads.

Combine butter with shallots, oregano and sugar in a large shallow dish, cover, cook on HIGH for 2 minutes. Stir in octopuses, wine, undrained crushed tomatoes and tomato paste, cover, cook on MEDIUM for about 25 minutes or until octopuses are tender.

Serves 4.

CHILLI FISH WITH CASHEW CURRY SAUCE

We used skinless, boneless bream fillets; recipe unsuitable to freeze.

60g butter
4 white fish fillets
1 small fresh red chilli, chopped
1 clove garlic, crushed
1 tablespoon chopped fresh chives
2 teaspoons curry powder
1 cup unroasted, unsalted cashew nuts
½ cup plain yoghurt

Melt butter in a large shallow dish on HIGH for 1 minute. Cut fish into 6cm strips, add to dish with chilli, garlic, chives, curry powder and nuts, cover, cook on HIGH for about 4 minutes or until fish is tender. Stir in yoghurt, cover, cook on MEDIUM for about 1 minute or until heated through.

Serves 4.

FISH WITH GINGER AND CHIVE SAUCE

We used skinless, boneless bream fillets. Recipe unsuitable to freeze.

30g butter
1 teaspoon grated fresh ginger
1 tablespoon chopped fresh chives
4 white fish fillets
1 tablespoon lemon juice
¼ cup dry white wine
2 teaspoons cornflour
½ cup water

Combine butter, ginger and chives in a large shallow dish, cover, cook on HIGH for 1 minute. Add fish in single layer, add juice and wine, cover, cook on HIGH for 5 minutes; remove fish.

Add blended cornflour and water to dish, cover, cook on HIGH for about 2 minutes or until mixture boils and thickens. Serve immediately over fish.

Serves 4.

SATAY PRAWNS

Recipe unsuitable to freeze.

1kg uncooked king prawns, shelled
¼ cup crunchy peanut butter
1 tablespoon light soya sauce
2 teaspoons chilli sauce
1 medium red pepper, sliced

Devein prawns, leaving tails intact. Combine peanut butter and sauces, add pepper and prawns, mix well. Cover dish, cook on MEDIUM HIGH for about 8 minutes or until prawns are tender; stir occasionally.

Serves 4.

BELOW: Herbed Octopuses in Red Wine Sauce. RIGHT: Clockwise from top: Satay Prawns; Fish with Ginger and Chive Sauce; Chilli Fish with Cashew Curry Sauce.

Bowl: Villa Italiana; tiles: Country Floors

Plates: Made in Japan; tiles: Country Floors

SEAFOOD

GARLIC PARMESAN MUSSELS

Recipe unsuitable to freeze.

1kg mussels
1 cup dry white wine
2 tablespoons oil
1 teaspoon grated lemon rind
1 tablespoon lemon juice
1 clove garlic, crushed
¼ cup grated parmesan cheese
1 tablespoon chopped fresh parsley

Clean mussels, remove beards. Place wine in a large shallow dish, cover, cook on HIGH for 4 minutes. Add mussels, cover, cook on HIGH for 4 minutes, remove mussels as they open. Discard any that do not open.

Remove mussels from shells, pull

China & fork: Limoges

Dish: Limoges; tiles: Country Floors

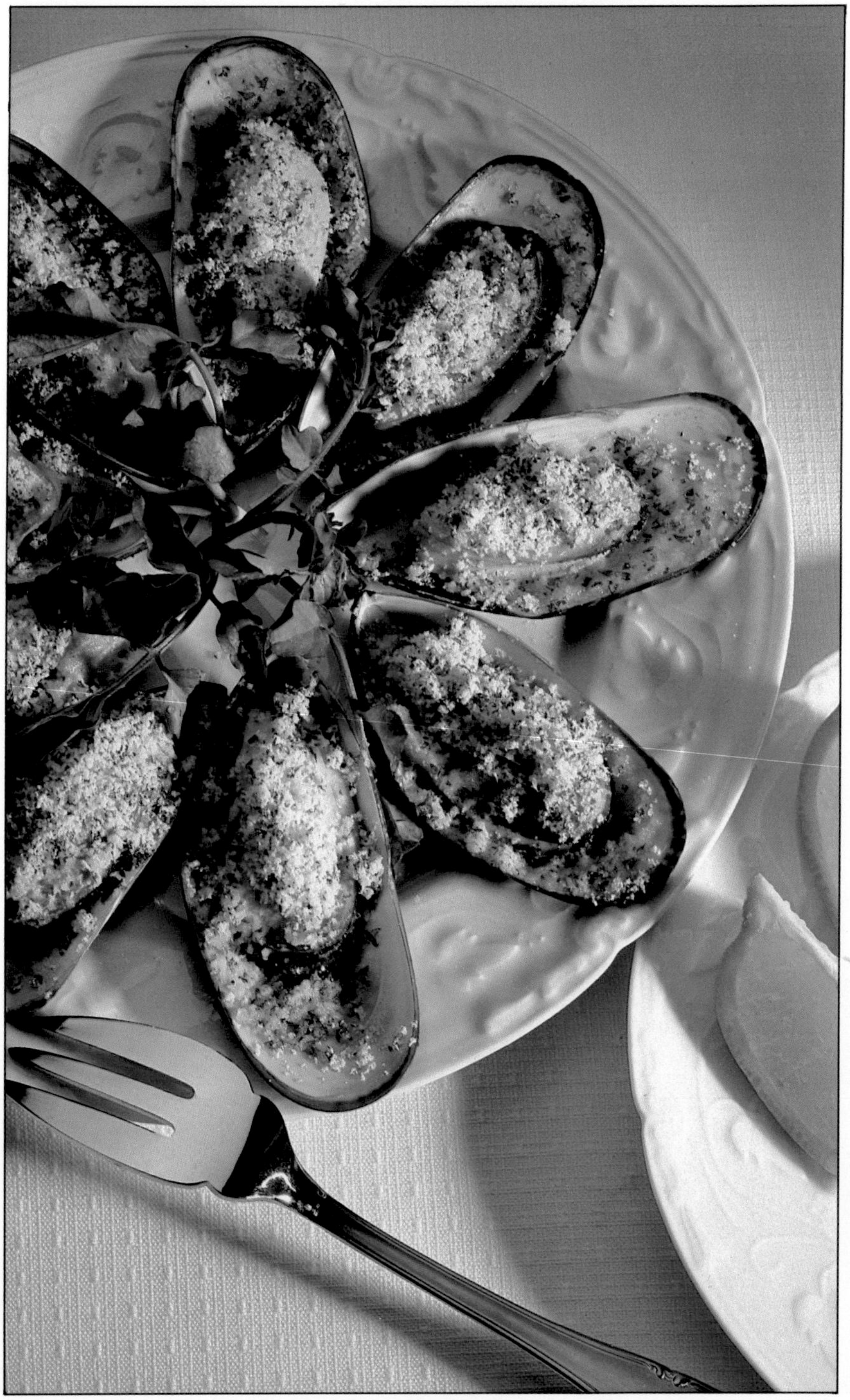

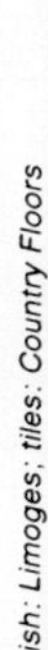

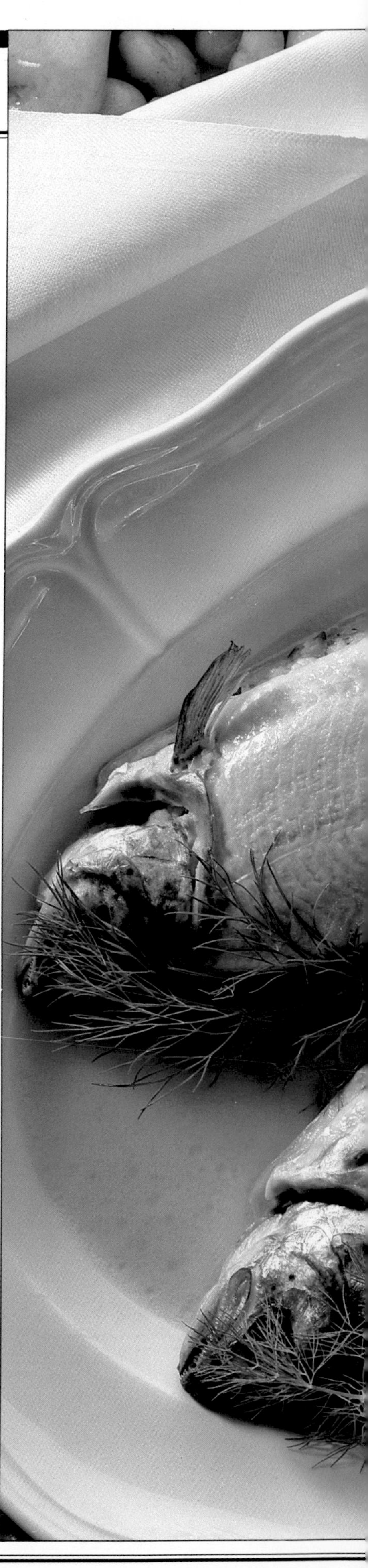

shells apart and discard half of each shell. Arrange mussel shells in a single layer on a flat dish, return mussels to shells. Brush each mussel with combined oil, lemon rind and juice and garlic. Sprinkle with cheese and parsley, cook on HIGH for 1 minute.

Serves 4.

FRESH HERB AND PRAWN SEASONED TROUT

Trout can be prepared up to a day before required. Recipe unsuitable to freeze.

60g butter
1 cup stale breadcrumbs
250g uncooked prawns, shelled, chopped
1 teaspoon grated lemon rind
1 tablespoon lemon juice
2 teaspoons chopped fresh parsley
1 teaspoon chopped fresh chives
1 teaspoon chopped fresh thyme
1 teaspoon chopped fresh dill
1 egg, lightly beaten
4 whole trout
½ cup lemon juice, extra
90g butter, extra

Melt butter in bowl on HIGH for 1 minute, stir in breadcrumbs, prawns, lemon rind, lemon juice, herbs and egg. Spoon seasoning into the cavity of each trout.

Cook 2 trout at a time. Place trout in a single layer in a large shallow dish, add half the extra lemon juice, and 30g of the extra butter, cover, cook on HIGH for 6 minutes, turn trout over half way through cooking. Stand 5 minutes after removing from oven.

Carefully remove skin from trout; place trout on serving plates. Whisk half the remaining butter into the liquid in the dish, serve lemon butter over trout. Repeat with remaining trout, extra lemon juice and extra butter.

Serves 4.

LEFT: Fresh Herb and Prawn Seasoned Trout. FAR LEFT: Garlic Parmesan Mussels.

SEAFOOD MARINARA

We used whiting fillets in this recipe. You will need to cook about 250g spaghetti or fettucine to serve with the marinara. Recipe unsuitable to freeze.

250g uncooked king prawns, shelled
2 white fish fillets
30g butter
1 medium onion, chopped
1 clove garlic, crushed
425g can tomatoes
¼ cup dry white wine
¼ cup water
1 tablespoon tomato paste
2 tablespoons cornflour
2 tablespoons water, extra
250g scallops
1 tablespoon chopped fresh parsley
1 tablespoon chopped fresh basil

Devein prawns, cut prawns and fish into bite-sized pieces.

Combine butter, onion and garlic in large shallow dish, cover, cook on HIGH for 3 minutes. Add undrained crushed tomatoes, wine, water and tomato paste, cover, cook on HIGH for 10 minutes.

Stir in blended cornflour and extra water, cook on HIGH for about 1 minute or until mixture boils and thickens.

Combine prawns, scallops and fish in a shallow dish, cover, cook on HIGH for about 3 minutes or until seafood is just tender; stir several times during cooking, drain.

Stir seafood into hot tomato sauce with herbs. Serve with hot pasta.

Serves 4.

China: Limoges; background laminate: Abet Laminati

Bowl: Villa Italiana; tiles: Pazotti

FISH IN CURRIED SAUCE

We used skinless gemfish fillets in this recipe. Recipe unsuitable to freeze.

750g white fish fillets
30g butter
1 medium onion, sliced
1 clove garlic, crushed
125g baby mushrooms, sliced
425g can tomatoes
1 teaspoon light soya sauce
2 teaspoons curry powder
½ teaspoon ground coriander
1 tablespoon chopped fresh parsley

CRAB AND BLACK BEAN SAUCE

Sake is a Japanese rice wine; dry sherry can be substituted. Recipe unsuitable to freeze.

4 uncooked blue swimmer crabs
2 tablespoons oil
¼ teaspoon sesame oil
1 medium onion, sliced
1 teaspoon grated fresh ginger
1 clove garlic, crushed
1 small fresh red chilli, chopped
2 tablespoons black bean sauce
1 tablespoon water
1 tablespoon sake
2 teaspoons cornflour
1 tablespoon water, extra

Remove large claws from crabs, cut bodies in half. Place oils, onion, ginger, garlic and chilli in a large shallow dish, cover, cook on HIGH for 2 minutes. Add crab pieces, black bean sauce, water and sake, cover, cook on HIGH for about 8 minutes or until crab shells turn red in colour; stir occasionally. Place crab onto serving plate.

Blend cornflour with extra water, add to dish, cook on HIGH for about 2 minutes or until sauce boils and thickens. Serve sauce over crab.

Serves 4.

BELOW: Fish in Curried Sauce.
LEFT: Crab and Black Bean Sauce.
FAR LEFT: Seafood Marinara.

Cut fish into bite-sized pieces. Combine butter, onion and garlic in a large shallow dish, cover, cook on HIGH for 3 minutes. Stir in fish, mushrooms, undrained crushed tomatoes, soya sauce, curry powder and coriander, cover, cook on HIGH for about 8 minutes or until fish is just tender; stir occasionally. Sprinkle with parsley.

Serves 4.

China: Pillivuyt from The Bay Tree

TOMATO FISH WITH CORIANDER RICE

We used skinless, boneless bream fillets. Recipe unsuitable to freeze.

8 small white fish fillets
30g butter
1 medium onion, chopped
1 clove garlic, crushed
425g can tomatoes
2 tablespoons tomato paste
2 teaspoons brown sugar
2 tablespoons chopped fresh parsley
CORIANDER RICE
1 cup basmati rice
2 cups hot water
2 chicken stock cubes, crumbled
1 teaspoon ground coriander

Fold fish in half, hold with toothpicks.

Combine butter, onion and garlic in a large shallow dish, cover, cook on HIGH for 3 minutes. Purée undrained tomatoes in blender or processor until smooth; strain. Add to onion mixture with tomato paste, sugar and parsley.

Add fish in a single layer, cover, cook on HIGH for about 4 minutes or until fish is tender; baste occasionally with tomato mixture during cooking. Serve with coriander rice.

Coriander Rice: Combine rice, water, stock cubes and coriander, cook on HIGH for about 15 minutes or until all the water is absorbed. Cover with foil while cooking fish.

Serves 4.

Dish: Limoges from Studio-Haus; fish server: Studio-Haus; tiles: Pazotti

China: Limoges from Studio-Haus; tiles: Pazotti

MUSTARD TROUT WITH LEMON AND DILL

Recipe unsuitable to freeze.

⅓ cup olive oil
1 tablespoon French mustard
1 clove garlic, crushed
2 tablespoons lemon juice
4 whole trout
1 tablespoon chopped fresh dill

Combine oil, mustard, garlic and lemon juice; brush over each trout, cover, refrigerate 4 hours or overnight.

Place 2 of the trout in a single layer in a shallow dish, cover, cook on HIGH for about 6 minutes or until trout are

tender; carefully remove skin. To serve, spoon liquid over trout, sprinkle with dill.

Repeat with remaining trout.

Serves 4.

ABOVE: Left: Fish in Basil Cream Sauce; right: Tomato Fish with Coriander Rice. LEFT: Mustard Trout with Lemon and Dill.

FISH IN BASIL CREAM SAUCE

We used skinless, boneless flathead fillets. Recipe unsuitable to freeze.

15g butter
1 tablespoon chopped fresh basil
½ cup cream
1½ tablespoons grated parmesan cheese
2 tablespoons dry vermouth
8 small white fish fillets

Combine butter, basil, cream, cheese and vermouth in a large shallow dish, cook on HIGH for 2 minutes. Add fish in a single layer, cook, covered, on HIGH for about 5 minutes or until fish is just tender.

Serves 4.

PEPPERED FISH WITH HERBED BUTTER

We used kingfish steaks in this recipe; it is unsuitable to freeze.

4 white fish steaks
freshly ground black pepper
60g butter
1 tablespoon lemon juice
1 tablespoon chopped fresh parsley
1 teaspoon chopped fresh thyme

Sprinkle steaks with pepper. Combine butter, lemon juice and herbs in a large shallow dish, cook on HIGH for 1 minute. Add fish in a single layer, cover, cook on HIGH for about 5 minutes or until fish is tender.

Serves 4.

SAUCY SCALLOPS WITH LEMON SESAME TOPPING

Recipe unsuitable to freeze.

500g scallops
2 tablespoons lemon juice
30g butter
1 tablespoon lemon butter
1 clove garlic, crushed
2 teaspoons sugar
1 small chicken stock cube, crumbled
1 tablespoon cornflour
¼ cup water
½ cup cream

SESAME TOPPING

¼ cup packaged breadcrumbs
1 tablespoon sesame seeds
15g butter
1 tablespoon chopped fresh parsley

Place scallops in a single layer in a large shallow dish, cover, cook on HIGH for 2 minutes, drain; return scallops to dish.

Combine lemon juice, butter, lemon butter, garlic, sugar and stock cube in a small bowl, cook on HIGH for 1 minute, stir in blended cornflour, water and cream, cook on HIGH for about 2 minutes or until sauce boils and thickens; stir occasionally. Pour sauce over scallops, sprinkle with topping, cook on HIGH for about 30 seconds or until heated through.

Sesame Topping: Combine all ingredients in a bowl, cook on HIGH for 2 minutes, stirring occasionally.

Serves 4.

LOBSTER IN LIME BUTTER

Any citrus rind and juice can be substituted for the lime. Recipe unsuitable to freeze.

4 uncooked lobster tails
60g butter
1 clove garlic, crushed
4 green shallots, chopped
¼ cup pine nuts
2 teaspoons grated lime rind
2 tablespoons lime juice
½ teaspoon sugar

Remove lobster flesh from shells, cut flesh into 1cm slices. Combine butter, garlic, shallots, pine nuts and rind in a large shallow dish, cook on HIGH for 1½ minutes, stirring halfway through cooking time.

Add lobster to dish in single layer with juice and sugar, mix well, cover, cook on MEDIUM for about 8 minutes or until lobster is just tender, stir occasionally during cooking.

Serves 4.

China: Limoges

LEFT: Lobster in Lime Butter. RIGHT: Top: Peppered Fish with Herbed Butter; bottom: Saucy Scallops with Lemon Sesame Topping.

SALMON AND ASPARAGUS FRITTATA

Recipe unsuitable to freeze.

210g can red salmon, drained
310g can asparagus cuts, drained
1 medium onion, chopped
4 eggs, lightly beaten
½ cup grated tasty cheese
1 tablespoon chopped fresh dill
1 teaspoon curry powder

Combine all ingredients in a large bowl, mix well, pour into a greased 23cm pie dish, cover, cook on MEDIUM for about 12 minutes or until almost set. Stand 5 minutes before serving.

SESAME HONEY SQUID

Recipe unsuitable to freeze.

500g small squid hoods
¼ cup light soya sauce
2 tablespoons dry sherry
1 tablespoon honey
1 teaspoon sesame oil
2 teaspoons grated fresh ginger
1 clove garlic, crushed
1 tablespoon oil
1 medium onion, quartered
1 medium red pepper, thinly sliced
2 teaspoons cornflour
1 tablespoon water
1 tablespoon sesame seeds, toasted

Using a sharp knife, cut a diamond pattern inside squid; do not cut through. Cut squid into squares.

Combine soya sauce, sherry, honey, sesame oil, ginger and garlic in bowl, add squid, cover, refrigerate several hours or overnight.

Remove squid from marinade; reserve marinade. Place oil in a large shallow dish, heat on HIGH for 1 minute, add squid, onion and pepper, cook on HIGH for about 4 minutes or until squid is tender; stir occasionally.

Combine blended cornflour and water with reserved marinade, add to dish, cook on HIGH for about 2 minutes or until mixture boils and thickens. Serve the squid sprinkled with sesame seeds.

Serves 4.

Dish: Studio-Haus

Background laminate: Abet Laminati

China: Limoges; background laminate: Abet Laminati

ABOVE: Sweet and Sour Prawn and Pepper Kebabs. LEFT: Sesame Honey Squid. FAR LEFT: Salmon and Asparagus Frittata.

SWEET AND SOUR PRAWN AND PEPPER KEBABS

Soak bamboo skewers in cold water for at least 1 hour before using to prevent burning during cooking. Sauce can be made a day ahead. Recipe unsuitable to freeze.

750g uncooked king prawns, shelled
1 medium red pepper, chopped
1 medium green pepper, chopped
1 medium onion, chopped
225g can pineapple pieces, drained
SWEET AND SOUR SAUCE
3 teaspoons cornflour
¾ cup water
1 teaspoon light soya sauce
2 tablespoons tomato sauce
2 tablespoons brown sugar
1½ tablespoons brown vinegar

Devein prawns, leaving tails intact. Thread prawns, peppers, onion and pineapple onto skewers. Arrange skewers in a single layer in a large shallow dish, cook on HIGH for about 5 minutes or until prawns are just tender. Serve with sweet and sour sauce.

Sweet and Sour Sauce: Combine blended cornflour and water with remaining ingredients in bowl, cook on HIGH for about 3 minutes or until sauce boils and thickens.

Serves 4.

LAYERED SEAFOOD TERRINE

Use any type of boneless, skinless fish for this recipe. Terrine can be prepared up to 1 day ahead. Recipe unsuitable to freeze.

500g white fish fillets
250g scallops
500g cooked prawns, shelled
1 egg
2 egg whites
6 green shallots, chopped
2 teaspoons grated fresh ginger
½ cup stale breadcrumbs
1 tablespoon chopped fresh parsley
CREAMY SHALLOT SAUCE
300g carton sour cream
2 green shallots, chopped
1 teaspoon chopped fresh dill
2 teaspoons mayonnaise

Blend or process fish, half the scallops, half the prawns, egg and egg whites until smooth; stir in shallots, ginger, breadcrumbs and parsley.

Lightly grease a loaf dish (14cm x 21cm). Arrange half the remaining scallops and prawns over the base of the dish, top with half the fish mixture, place remaining scallops and prawns over fish mixture, top with remaining fish mixture.

Cover, cook on MEDIUM for about 20 minutes or until terrine feels slightly firm. Stand 5 minutes before serving hot or cold with cold sauce.

Creamy Shallot Sauce: Combine all ingredients in a bowl; mix well.

Serves 4.

TUNA BROCCOLI MORNAY

Recipe unsuitable to freeze.

125g broccoli
125g cauliflower
1 medium red pepper, chopped
60g butter
2 tablespoons plain flour
1 cup milk
½ cup cream
½ cup grated tasty cheese
425g can tuna, drained
15g butter, extra
½ cup packaged breadcrumbs
1 tablespoon chopped fresh parsley
pinch paprika

Break broccoli and cauliflower into flowerets, place in a large shallow dish with pepper, cover, cook on HIGH for 3 minutes; drain.

Melt butter in the same dish on HIGH for 1 minute, stir in flour then milk, cook on HIGH for about 2 minutes or until mixture boils and thickens; stir occasionally. Stir in cream and cheese, then vegetables and tuna.

Melt extra butter in a small bowl on HIGH for 15 seconds, stir in crumbs, parsley and paprika. Sprinkle over tuna mixture, cook on HIGH for about 5 minutes or until heated through.

Serves 4.

FISH CUTLETS WITH MUSHROOM PARSLEY SAUCE

We used jewfish cutlets. Recipe unsuitable to freeze.

15g butter
3 green shallots, chopped
1 clove garlic, chopped
2 teaspoons plain flour
¾ cup dry white wine
1 medium tomato, finely chopped
125g baby mushrooms, chopped
¼ cup cream
4 white fish cutlets
1 tablespoon chopped fresh parsley

Combine butter, shallots and garlic in a large shallow dish, cover, cook on HIGH for 1 minute. Stir in flour then wine, tomato, mushrooms and cream. Cook on HIGH for about 3 minutes or until mixture boils and thickens; stir occasionally. Add fish in single layer to the mushroom mixture, cover, cook on HIGH for about 5 minutes or until fish is tender. Sprinkle with parsley.

Serves 4.

BELOW: Layered Seafood Terrine. RIGHT: Top: Tuna Broccoli Mornay; bottom: Fish Cutlets with Mushroom Parsley Sauce.

Dish: Pillivuyt from The Bay Tree; tiles: Pazotti

Dishes: Pillivuyt from The Bay Tree; cutlery: Studio-Haus; tiles: Pazotti

BEEF & VEAL

Tender lean cuts of beef and veal are quickly transformed into many tempting, satisfying dishes. Always remove any fat and sinew from the meat and do not overcook or the meat will become tough and dry. Some of these recipes can be cooked ahead and frozen for future use; others are at their best when prepared, cooked and served immediately.

VEAL STROGANOFF LOAF WITH MUSHROOM SAUCE

Loaf can be frozen for up to 2 months.

750g stewing veal
250g sausage mince
40g packet Beef Stroganoff Sauce Mix
4 green shallots, chopped
1 egg, lightly beaten
2 tablespoons tomato paste
MUSHROOM SAUCE
30g butter
375g mushrooms, sliced
½ cup cream
1 tablespoon grated parmesan cheese
½ teaspoon paprika
2 teaspoons cornflour
1 tablespoon water
1 tablespoon chopped fresh parsley
¼ cup coarsely grated fresh parmesan cheese

Process veal until finely minced, combine in a bowl with sausage mince, dry sauce mix, shallots, egg and tomato paste; mix well. Press mixture into a 12cm x 22cm loaf dish. Cook on HIGH for 8 minutes. Turn loaf out onto a rack, place on rack in a shallow dish. Cook on HIGH for about 10 minutes or until loaf is cooked through; sprinkle with cheese, serve with mushroom sauce.

Mushroom Sauce: Combine butter and mushrooms in a shallow dish, cook on HIGH for about 2 minutes or until mushrooms are tender. Add cream, cheese, paprika and blended cornflour and water, cook on HIGH for about 3 minutes or until mixture boils and thickens, stir occasionally, stir in parsley.

Serves 4.

CHILLI CORIANDER VEAL

Recipe unsuitable to freeze.

4 veal steaks (schnitzels)
2 tablespoons light soya sauce
1 tablespoon chilli sauce
1 small fresh red chilli, chopped
2 teaspoons chopped fresh coriander
1 tablespoon cornflour
¼ cup water
1 small beef stock cube, crumbled

Combine veal, sauces, chilli and coriander in a bowl, cover, refrigerate for at least 1 hour (overnight is better).

Place veal in a single layer in a large shallow dish, cover, cook on HIGH for 3 minutes on each side.

Blend cornflour with water, stir into dish with stock cube, cover, cook on HIGH for about 2 minutes or until sauce boils and thickens; stir occasionally. Serve immediately.

Serves 4.

From left: Chilli Coriander Veal; Veal Stroganoff Loaf with Mushroom Sauce.

Plate: Studio-Haus; platter: Modern Living

CHILLI MEATBALLS IN TOMATO SAUCE

Uncooked meatballs in their sauce can be frozen for up to 2 months.

500g minced beef
4 green shallots, chopped
1 clove garlic, crushed
1 tablespoon tomato paste
½ cup stale breadcrumbs
2 tablespoons chopped fresh parsley
1 egg, lightly beaten
plain flour
425g can tomatoes
½ teaspoon chilli powder
4 green shallots, chopped, extra
1 teaspoon Worcestershire sauce
2 tablespoons dry white wine

Combine mince, shallots, garlic, tomato paste, breadcrumbs, parsley and egg in a large bowl, mix well. Shape mixture into 8 meatballs; toss lightly in flour. Place meatballs in a single layer in a shallow dish.

Combine undrained crushed tomatoes, chilli powder, extra shallots, sauce and wine in a bowl, pour over meatballs, cover, cook on MEDIUM for 20 minutes, remove cover, cook on MEDIUM for about 10 minutes or until meatballs are tender. Change position of meatballs halfway through cooking time. Serve immediately.

Serves 4.

BEEF STROGANOFF SLICE

Recipe unsuitable to freeze.

500g minced beef
40g packet Beef Stroganoff Sauce Mix
⅓ cup tomato sauce
1 tablespoon barbecue sauce
1 egg, lightly beaten

CHEESY BACON FILLING
1 tablespoon chopped fresh parsley
250g cottage cheese
2 bacon rashers, chopped
250g packet frozen spinach, thawed, drained
1 egg, lightly beaten

CRUMB TOPPING
1 tablespoon chopped fresh parsley
2 tablespoons stale breadcrumbs
15g butter, melted
2 tablespoons grated tasty cheese
pinch paprika

Combine beef, dry stroganoff sauce mix, sauces and egg in a bowl; mix well. Press over base of a greased rectangular dish (8 cup capacity), cover, cook on HIGH for 3 minutes.

Spread filling into dish, cover, cook on HIGH for 12 minutes. Sprinkle with topping, cook on HIGH for 2 minutes. Stand, covered, for 10 minutes before serving in slices.

Cheesy Bacon Filling: Combine all ingredients in a bowl; mix well.

Crumb Topping: Combine all ingredients in a bowl; mix well.

Serves 4.

BELOW: Chilli Meatballs in Tomato Sauce. RIGHT: Beef Stroganoff Slice.

China: Studio-Haus

Lantern: Modern Living; napkin: Studio-Haus

BEEF 'N' ONION BURGERS

Uncooked crumbed burgers can be frozen for up to 2 months.

15g butter
1 small onion, finely chopped
500g minced beef
1 teaspoon paprika
2 tablespoons tomato sauce
1 egg, lightly beaten
2 tablespoons fruit chutney
pinch dried mixed herbs
¼ cup packaged breadcrumbs
45g packet French Onion Soup Mix
2 tablespoons packaged breadcrumbs, extra

Combine butter and onion in a large bowl, cover, cook on HIGH for 3 minutes. Stir in mince, paprika, tomato sauce, egg, chutney, herbs and breadcrumbs. Shape mixture into 8 patties.

Combine dry soup mix and extra breadcrumbs, press the patties into this mixture.

Place patties in single layer on a large flat dish. Cook on MEDIUM HIGH for about 5 minutes or until burgers are firm; turn once during the cooking time. Serve immediately.

Makes 8.

HONEYED VEAL WITH SPINACH

The nut of veal is a boneless piece of meat cut from the leg; however, thick veal steaks or cutlets can be substituted. Recipe unsuitable to freeze.

750g nut of veal
2 teaspoons honey
1 tablespoon light soya sauce
½ teaspoon ground cumin
3 green shallots, chopped
1 tablespoon oil
1 tablespoon cornflour
¼ cup water
1 bunch English spinach (40 leaves)

Cut veal into chunks, combine with honey, soya sauce, cumin and shallots in a large bowl, cover, stand at least 30 minutes (overnight is better).

Heat oil in a large shallow dish, add veal mixture, cover, cook on HIGH for about 7 minutes or until veal is almost tender; stir occasionally.

Blend cornflour with water, stir into veal, cover, cook on HIGH for about 2 minutes or until the mixture boils and thickens.

Place spinach in a large bowl, cover, cook on HIGH for about 2 minutes or until spinach is just wilted. Place spinach on serving plate, top with veal; serve immediately.

Serves 4.

China: Studio-Haus; table & photo frames: Modern Living

From left: Beef 'n' Onion Burgers; Honeyed Veal with Spinach.

China: Studio-Haus

Bowl: Hampshire & Lowndes

SPICY PEPPERED STEAK

It is easier to cut the steak finely if it is partly frozen. Recipe can be frozen for up to 2 months.

1½ tablespoons coarsely ground fresh black pepper
750g topside steak
1 small red pepper, sliced
1 small green pepper, chopped
6 green shallots, chopped
1½ tablespoons cornflour
½ cup water
3 teaspoons grated fresh ginger
3 cloves garlic, crushed
2 tablespoons light soya sauce
1 teaspoon sesame oil

Sprinkle black pepper evenly on both sides of steak and press pepper firmly onto steak. Cut steak into wafer thin slices.

Combine steak with peppers and shallots in a large shallow dish. Blend cornflour with water, stir in ginger, garlic, soya sauce and sesame oil; add to steak; mix well. Cover dish, cook on HIGH for 10 minutes, stir occasionally. Reduce to MEDIUM, cook for about 10 minutes or until steak is tender, stir occasionally. Serve immediately.

Serves 4.

CHILLI AND GINGER BEEF

It is easier to cut steak when partly frozen. Recipe unsuitable to freeze.

1 tablespoon oil
2 small leeks, sliced
1 teaspoon grated fresh ginger
1 clove garlic, crushed
2 small fresh red chillies, chopped
500g beef eye fillet steak, finely sliced
1 tablespoon dark soya sauce
1 tablespoon oyster sauce
2 teaspoons cornflour
2 tablespoons water

Combine oil with leeks, ginger, garlic and chillies in a large shallow dish, cover, cook on HIGH for 5 minutes. Add steak and sauces, cover, cook on HIGH for about 5 minutes or until tender. Stir in blended cornflour and water, cover, cook on HIGH for about 3 minutes or until mixture boils and thickens; stir occasionally.

Serves 4.

ABOVE: Veal and Bacon Casserole; LEFT: Top: Chilli and Ginger Beef; bottom: Spicy Peppered Steak.

VEAL AND BACON CASSEROLE

Casserole can be frozen for up to 2 months. Thaw in refrigerator overnight.

30g butter
1 medium onion, finely sliced
2 medium potatoes, thinly sliced
3 bacon rashers, chopped
500g veal steaks (schnitzels)
3 tablespoons gravy powder
½ cup water
1 beef stock cube, crumbled

Combine butter, onion, potatoes and bacon in a large shallow dish, cover, cook on HIGH for 4 minutes.

Cut veal into 2cm pieces, add to onion mixture, cover, cook on HIGH for about 5 minutes or until tender; stir occasionally. Stir in blended gravy powder and water and stock cube. Cook on HIGH for about 3 minutes or until mixture boils and thickens; stir occasionally during cooking.

Serves 4.

PASTA & RICE

Cooking time for pasta will vary depending on heat of the water and type of pasta used. Fresh pasta will take the least time to cook; packaged pasta the longest. Rice, as a rule, needs double the amount of water to rice; however, 1 cup brown rice needs 2½ cups water. White rice takes about 15 minutes to cook; brown rice about 25 minutes. Use a large shallow dish about 4cm deep for best results. Do not cover rice or pasta while cooking, but do stir at least twice during cooking.

CREAMY SALMON AND MUSHROOM FETTUCINE

Recipe unsuitable to freeze.

200g fettucine (pasta)
1 litre (4 cups) hot water
30g butter
200g mushrooms, sliced
2 green shallots, chopped
210g can salmon, drained, flaked
⅓ cup cream
1 egg, lightly beaten
½ cup grated tasty cheese
1 tablespoon chopped fresh parsley

Place pasta in a large shallow dish with the water, cook on HIGH for about 10 minutes or until pasta is just tender, stir occasionally. Stand a few minutes before draining. Combine butter, mushrooms and shallots in a large bowl, cook on HIGH for 2 minutes. Stir in pasta and remaining ingredients. Cook on MEDIUM for 5 minutes or until heated through; stir occasionally.

Serves 4.

SPICY BROWN RICE RING

Rice ring can be prepared up to a day ahead. Recipe unsuitable to freeze.

1 cup brown rice
2½ cups hot water
30g butter
1 small fresh red chilli, chopped
1 clove garlic, crushed
3 green shallots, chopped
¼ teaspoon curry powder
¼ teaspoon ground cumin
¼ teaspoon ground coriander
¼ teaspoon ground cardamom
2 sticks celery, finely chopped
1 medium carrot, finely chopped
½ cup chopped pecans or walnuts
⅓ cup sour cream

Place rice in a large shallow dish, add water, cook on HIGH for 25 minutes, stir occasionally, cover, allow to stand 5 minutes.

Combine butter, chilli, garlic, shallots and spices in large bowl, cover, cook on HIGH for 2 minutes. Add celery and carrot to bowl, cover, cook on HIGH for about 3 minutes or until carrot is tender. Stir rice into vegetable mixture with nuts and cream. Press mixture into a 20cm ring dish, cool, refrigerate several hours before serving.

Serves 4.

GINGERED PORK WITH PASTA

Recipe unsuitable to freeze.

200g (2½ cups) pasta
1 litre (4 cups) hot water
1 tablespoon oil
2 medium onions, sliced
2 teaspoons grated fresh ginger
1 clove garlic, crushed
400g pork fillets, sliced thinly
2 teaspoons cornflour
¼ cup water, extra
1 tablespoon hoisin sauce
2 teaspoons dark soya sauce
1 tablespoon dry sherry
pinch five spice powder
4 green shallots, chopped

Place pasta in a large shallow dish with hot water. Cook on HIGH for about 10 minutes or until the pasta is just tender, stir occasionally. Stand a few minutes before draining.

Heat oil in a large bowl, add onions, ginger and garlic, cover, cook on HIGH for 3 minutes. Add pork, cook, covered, on HIGH for about 4 minutes or until pork is tender. Blend cornflour with extra water, sauces, sherry and five spice powder, stir into pork mixture, cook on HIGH for 2 minutes or until mixture boils and thickens, stir occasionally. Add shallots and pasta to pork mixture, cook on HIGH for 1 minute or until heated through.

Serves 4.

LEFT: Spicy Brown Rice Ring. RIGHT: Top: Creamy Salmon and Mushroom Fettucine; bottom: Gingered Pork with Pasta.

Tiles: C.O.D. Ceramics

SPINACH LASAGNE PIE

Recipe unsuitable to freeze.

9 instant lasagne sheets
1 tablespoon oil, approximately
½ cup grated parmesan cheese
2 tablespoons chopped fresh parsley
CHEESY SPINACH FILLING
15g butter
1 small onion, finely chopped
¼ teaspoon dried oregano leaves
250g packet frozen spinach
1 cup (200g) ricotta cheese
100g ham, chopped
2 eggs, lightly beaten
TOMATO PEPPERCORN SAUCE
15g butter
1 small onion, finely chopped
1 clove garlic, crushed
¼ teaspoon dried oregano leaves
310g can Tomato Supreme
2 teaspoons canned green peppercorns, drained, crushed

Place a single layer of lasagne sheets with a little of the oil in a large dish, cover with boiling water. Cover, cook on HIGH for 5 minutes, stand 5 minutes; drain. Repeat with remaining lasagne sheets.

Grease a 22cm pie plate, place 3 sheets of lasagne over base, top with half the filling. Repeat with remaining lasagne and filling, finishing with lasagne. Spread with sauce, sprinkle with combined cheese and parsley. Cook on MEDIUM for about 4 minutes or until heated through. Stand 10 minutes before serving.

Cheesy Spinach Filling: Combine butter, onion and oregano in a small bowl, cover, cook on HIGH for 3 minutes. Place spinach in a large bowl, cover, cook on HIGH for about 2 minutes or until soft, drain and squeeze out as much liquid as possible. Return spinach to bowl, stir in onion mixture, cheese, ham and eggs.

Tomato Peppercorn Sauce: Combine butter, onion, garlic and oregano in small bowl, cover, cook on HIGH for 3 minutes. Add Tomato Supreme and peppercorns, cover, cook on HIGH for about 1 minute or until heated through.

TAGLIATELLE WITH SMOKED SALMON SAUCE

We used spinach-flavoured tagliatelle in this recipe. Bocconcini are small, fresh Italian mozzarella cheeses; if unavailable, substitute mozzarella cheese. Recipe unsuitable to freeze.

China: Villeroy & Boch; tiles: C.O.D. Ceramics

China: Village Living; tiles: Japan Ceramics

200g tagliatelle (pasta)
1 litre (4 cups) hot water
SMOKED SALMON SAUCE
60g butter
2 small golden shallots, chopped
1 teaspoon chopped fresh thyme
250g smoked salmon, sliced
1 tablespoon brandy
1 tablespoon grated parmesan cheese
125g bocconcini, thinly sliced
¼ cup sour cream

Place pasta in a large shallow dish with hot water, cook on HIGH for about 10 minutes, stir occasionally. Stand a few minutes before draining.

Smoked Salmon Sauce: Combine butter, shallots and thyme in a large bowl, cover, cook on HIGH for 3 minutes. Add salmon and brandy, cover, cook on MEDIUM HIGH for 2 minutes. Stir in cheeses, cover, cook on MEDIUM HIGH for 3 minutes. Stir in pasta and cream, cover, cook on HIGH for about 2 minutes or until heated through.

Serves 4.

BROCCOLI AND FETTUCINE WITH WALNUT CREAM SAUCE

Recipe unsuitable to freeze.

200g fettucine (pasta)
1 litre (4 cups) hot water
500g broccoli
WALNUT CREAM SAUCE
¾ cup cream
½ cup coarsely grated fresh parmesan cheese
2 tablespoons chopped walnuts or pecans
2 teaspoons cornflour
2 tablespoons water

Place pasta in a large shallow dish with hot water, cook on HIGH for about 10 minutes or until pasta is just tender, stir occasionally. Stand a few minutes before draining.

Cut broccoli into flowerets, place in dish, cover, cook on HIGH for about 5 minutes. Place pasta on serving plate, top with broccoli and sauce.

Walnut Cream Sauce: Combine cream, cheese and walnuts in a bowl, cover, cook on HIGH for about 2 minutes. Stir in blended cornflour and water, cover, cook on HIGH for about 2 minutes or until sauce boils and thickens, stir occasionally.

Serves 4.

LEFT: Top: Tagliatelle with Smoked Salmon Sauce; bottom: Broccoli and Fettucine with Walnut Cream Sauce. FAR LEFT: Spinach Lasagne Pie.

FRESH HERB AND BEEF SAUCE WITH PASTA

Sauce can be frozen for up to 3 months.

500g minced beef
2 medium onions, chopped
2 sticks celery, chopped
1 clove garlic, crushed
425g can tomatoes
½ cup tomato paste
¼ cup dry red wine
2 tablespoons chopped fresh parsley
2 teaspoons chopped fresh oregano
2 teaspoons chopped fresh basil
1 teaspoon chopped fresh thyme
200g (2½ cups) pasta
1 litre (4 cups) hot water

Break mince into pieces, place mince into a large shallow dish, cook on HIGH for about 3 minutes, stir occasionally. Drain well.

Return mince to bowl with onions, celery and garlic. Cook on HIGH for 5 minutes, stir occasionally. Add undrained crushed tomatoes, tomato paste, wine and herbs. Cover, cook on HIGH for about 20 minutes or until mince is tender, stir occasionally.

Place pasta in a large bowl with the water, cook on HIGH for about 10 minutes or until pasta is just tender; stir occasionally. Stand a few minutes before draining. Serve with pasta.

Serves 4.

GINGER AND CASHEW RICE

Recipe can be prepared up to a day in advance. It is unsuitable to freeze.

1 cup long grain rice
2 cups hot water
30g butter
1 clove garlic, crushed
½ cup unroasted cashew nuts, chopped
¼ cup chopped glacé ginger
1 teaspoon grated lemon rind
¼ teaspoon ground cumin
2 tablespoons chopped fresh mint

Combine rice and water in a large shallow dish, cook on HIGH for 15 minutes; stir occasionally.

Combine butter, garlic and nuts in a dish, cook on HIGH for 2 minutes, stir occasionally. Stir in rice and remaining ingredients, cook on HIGH for about 3 minutes or until the mixture is heated through; stir occasionally.

Serves 4.

BELOW: Fresh Herb and Beef Sauce with Pasta. RIGHT: Ginger and Cashew Rice.

China: Limoges from Studio-Haus; tiles: Pazotti

Bowls: Village Living; table: Raw Straw

CREAMY HAM AND MUSHROOM PASTA

Recipe unsuitable to freeze.

30g butter
1 medium onion, chopped
1 clove garlic, crushed
125g ham, chopped
185g mushrooms, sliced
2 tablespoons plain flour
½ teaspoon dry mustard
1 cup milk
½ cup cream
½ cup grated tasty cheese
2 tablespoons grated parmesan cheese
2 tablespoons chopped fresh parsley
200g (2½ cups) pasta
1 litre (4 cups) hot water
1 teaspoon chopped fresh parsley, extra

Combine butter, onion, garlic and ham in a large shallow dish, cover, cook on HIGH for 3 minutes. Add mushrooms, cover, cook on HIGH for 3 minutes. Stir in flour and mustard, then milk and cream, cook on HIGH for about 7 minutes or until mixture boils and thickens. Stir in cheeses and parsley.

Place pasta in a large bowl with hot water, cook on HIGH for about 10 minutes or until pasta is just tender; stir occasionally. Stand a few minutes before draining. Stir pasta into ham and mushroom mixture, cover, cook on HIGH for about 1 minute or until heated through, sprinkle with extra parsley.

Serves 4.

SPICY CHICKEN AND HAM WITH SULTANA RICE

Recipe unsuitable to freeze.

30g butter
1 medium onion, chopped
185g ham, chopped
1 clove garlic, crushed
1 teaspoon curry powder
½ teaspoon turmeric
¼ teaspoon ground cumin
¼ cup sultanas
1 cup rice
2 cups hot water
1 small chicken stock cube, crumbled
3 chicken breast fillets, chopped
2 tablespoons chopped fresh parsley

Combine butter, onion, ham and garlic in a large shallow dish, cover, cook on

China: Studio-Haus; vase: Limoges from Lifestyle Imports

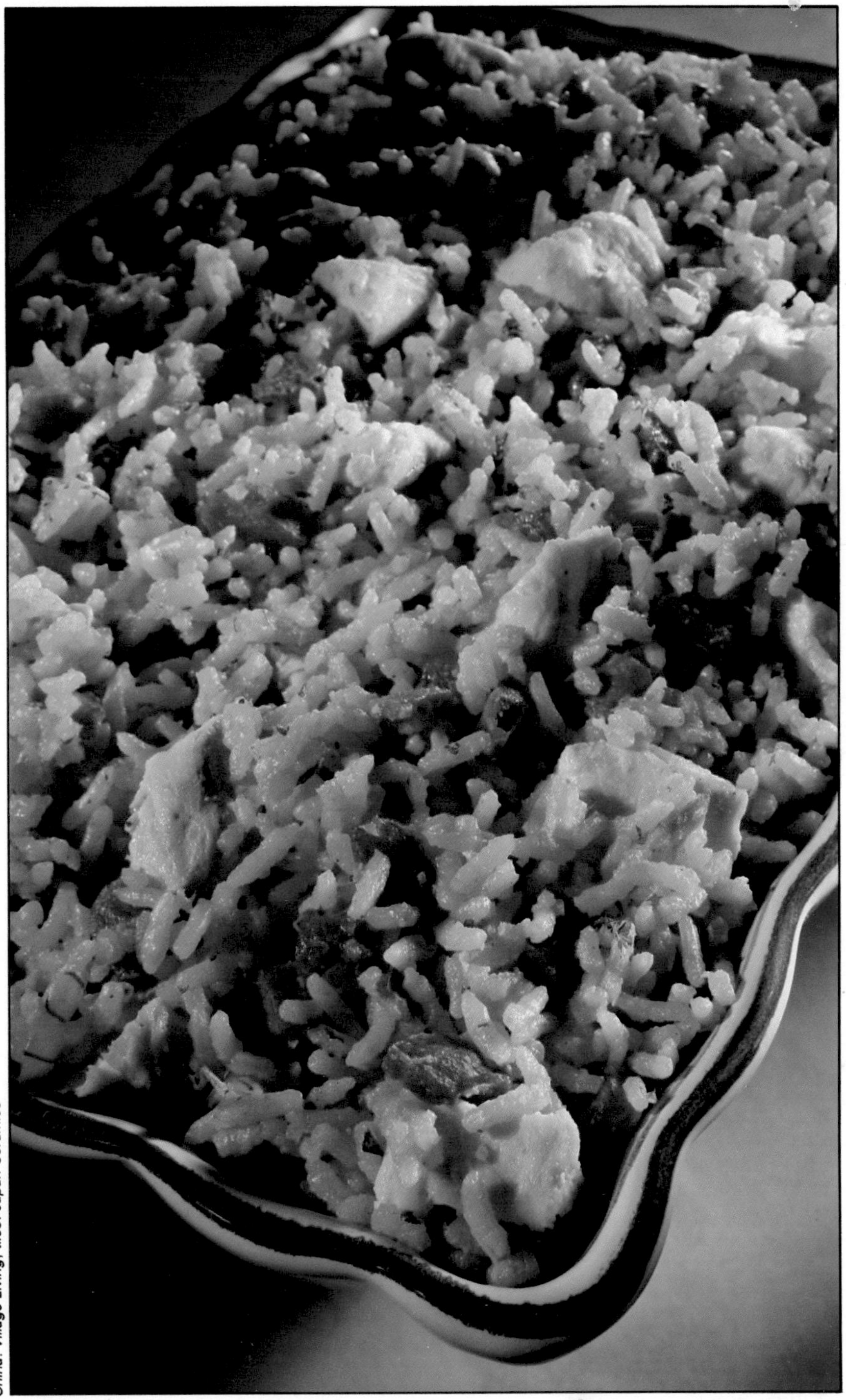

China: Village Living; tiles: Japan Ceramics

HIGH for 4 minutes. Add curry powder, turmeric, cumin and sultanas, cover, cook on HIGH for 1 minute. Stir in rice, pour in the water with the stock cube, cook on HIGH for 10 minutes, stir occasionally. Add chicken, cover, cook on HIGH for about 5 minutes or until chicken is tender, stir occasionally. Stir in parsley just before serving.

Serves 4.

LEFT: Creamy Ham and Mushroom Pasta. ABOVE: Spicy Chicken and Ham with Sultana Rice.

VEGETABLES

The colours and flavours of vegetables are superb when cooked in the microwave, but it is best to avoid using salt during cooking as it will toughen them. Cut vegetables to a uniform size for even cooking. Prepare vegetables by peeling or topping and tailing as usual.

China: Mikasa; tiles: Pazotti

CURRIED HONEY PUMPKIN

Recipe unsuitable to freeze.

500g butternut pumpkin
15g butter, chopped
1 teaspoon curry powder
½ teaspoon honey
2 tablespoons sultanas
2 teaspoons shredded coconut

Cut pumpkin into thin slices. Combine butter, curry powder, honey and sultanas in a large shallow dish, stir in pumpkin, cover, cook on HIGH for about 8 minutes or until pumpkin is tender; stir occasionally. Sprinkle with coconut, cook on HIGH for 2 minutes.

Serves 4.

FRESH BUTTERED MUSTARD CORN

Recipe unsuitable to freeze

2 large cobs fresh corn
1 tablespoon water
60g butter
2 teaspoons dry mustard
125g baby mushrooms, halved
1 medium red pepper, sliced
2 green shallots, coarsely chopped
1 tablespoon chopped fresh parsley

Cut corn into 1cm slices, place in a large bowl with the water, cover, cook on HIGH for about 5 minutes or until corn is tender; stir occasionally. Melt butter in a large shallow dish on HIGH for 1 minute. Add mustard, mushrooms, pepper and shallots, cover, cook on HIGH for 1 minute. Add corn, cover, cook on HIGH for about 1 minute or until heated through. Stir in parsley before serving.

Serves 4.

CREAMY CARROT RING

Recipe unsuitable to freeze.

1kg carrots, chopped
60g butter
4 green shallots, chopped
1 clove garlic, crushed
½ cup cream
3 eggs
1 cup grated tasty cheese
1 tablespoon chopped fresh parsley

Combine carrots, butter, shallots, garlic and cream in a large shallow dish, cover, cook on HIGH for about 20 minutes or until carrots are tender; cool.

Blend or process carrot mixture and eggs until smooth, stir in cheese and parsley. Pour mixture into a lightly greased 25cm ring dish (7 cup capacity). Cook on HIGH for about 10 minutes or until just set; stand 5 minutes before serving.

Serves 4.

Dishes: Pillivuyt from Zuhause

ABOVE: Left: Fresh Buttered Mustard Corn; right: Curried Honey Pumpkin. Left: Creamy Carrot Ring.

KUMARA WITH SOUR CREAM AND BACON

Recipe unsuitable to freeze

2 medium kumara
30g butter
1 medium onion, sliced
1 bacon rasher, sliced
1 tablespoon madeira or sherry
½ cup sour cream
2 tablespoons grated parmesan cheese

Cut kumara into 1cm thick lengths, place in a bowl of water. Combine butter, onion and bacon in a shallow dish, cover, cook on HIGH for 3 minutes. Add drained kumara, madeira, cream and cheese, cover, cook on HIGH for about 6 minutes or until tender.

Serves 4.

HOT ZUCCHINI MOUSSE

Recipe not suitable to freeze.

4 medium zucchini
1 teaspoon water
30g butter
1 medium onion, finely chopped
⅓ cup cream
2 eggs, lightly beaten
pinch nutmeg

Slice one zucchini thinly, place in a small bowl with the water, cover, cook on HIGH for 1 minute, place in cold water to cool; drain.

Lightly grease 4 dishes (half cup capacity), line sides with zucchini slices. Combine butter and onion in a bowl, cook on HIGH for 3 minutes. Chop remaining zucchini, add to onion mixture, cover, cook on HIGH for 5 minutes. Blend or process zucchini mixture until smooth, add cream, eggs and nutmeg, process until combined, pour into dishes. Cook on MEDIUM LOW for about 7 minutes or until mousses are set. Stand, covered, for 5 minutes before serving.

Serves 4.

RED PEPPER AND CUCUMBER SAUTE

Recipe unsuitable to freeze.

30g butter
1 small onion, chopped
1 clove garlic, crushed
1 medium red pepper, chopped
4 long thin green cucumbers, peeled, sliced
1 teaspoon lemon juice

Combine butter, onion and garlic in a bowl, cover, cook on HIGH for 3 minutes. Add pepper, cucumbers and lemon juice, cover, cook on HIGH for about 3 minutes or until hot.

Serves 4.

RIGHT: Top: Kumara with Sour Cream and Bacon; bottom: Red Pepper and Cucumber Saute. BELOW: Hot Zucchini Mousse.

Tiles: Pazotti

Dishes: Pillivuyt from Zuhause

VEGETABLES

BEAN AND PINE NUT SALAD

Recipe unsuitable to freeze.

500g green beans
2 tablespoons water
1 tablespoon oil
2 tablespoons pine nuts
1 tablespoon brown sugar
2 teaspoons lemon juice
250g punnet cherry tomatoes, halved

Combine beans and water in a large shallow dish, cover, cook on HIGH for 8 minutes, drain, return to dish.

Combine oil and pine nuts in a small bowl, cook on HIGH for about 4 minutes or until nuts are lightly browned, stir occasionally. Add pine nut mixture, sugar, lemon juice and tomatoes to beans, cover, cook on HIGH for about 2 minutes or until heated through.

Serves 4.

Spoon and cheese board: The Bay Tree; table: Freedom Furniture

ABOVE: Cheesy Vegetable Cups. BELOW: Spinach Salad with Hot Cider Dressing. RIGHT: Bean and Pine Nut Salad.

Bowl: The Bay Tree; tiles: Pazotti

Spoon: The Bay Tree

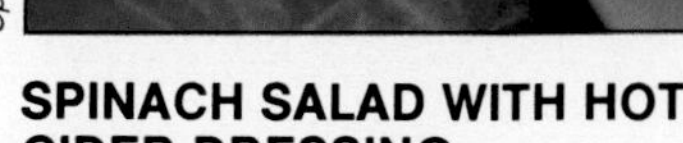

SPINACH SALAD WITH HOT CIDER DRESSING

Recipe unsuitable to freeze.

6 bacon rashers, chopped
1 bunch English spinach (40 leaves)
1 medium red pepper, finely chopped
CIDER DRESSING
1 tablespoon cider vinegar
1½ teaspoons sugar
1½ tablespoons water
2 tablespoons lemon juice
2 tablespoons oil

Place bacon in a shallow dish, cover, cook on HIGH for 3 minutes, drain, cook on HIGH for about 3 minutes or until crisp, drain on absorbent paper.

Tear spinach leaves into pieces. Place the spinach and pepper in serving bowl. Add hot dressing and sprinkle with bacon.

Cider Dressing: Combine vinegar, sugar, water and lemon juice in a small bowl, cover, cook on HIGH for 1 minute. Add oil, mix well.

Serves 4.

CHEESY VEGETABLE CUPS

Recipe unsuitable to freeze.

30g butter
1 medium onion, chopped
1 clove garlic, crushed
1 small zucchini, grated
1 small carrot, grated
60g baby mushrooms, sliced
1 cup grated tasty cheese
2 eggs, lightly beaten
2 tablespoons milk
2 tablespoons plain flour
1 tablespoon chopped fresh parsley

Combine butter, onion and garlic in a large bowl, cover, cook on HIGH for 3 minutes. Stir in zucchini, carrot, mushrooms, cheese, eggs, milk, flour and parsley. Spoon mixture into 4 dishes ($\frac{1}{2}$ cup capacity). Cook on HIGH for 5 minutes, stand 5 minutes before serving.

Serves 4.

CREAMY CARAWAY CABBAGE

Recipe unsuitable to freeze.

5 cups shredded red cabbage (about ¼ large cabbage)
1 tablespoon water
3 bacon rashers, chopped
1 medium onion, chopped
2 teaspoons caraway seeds
½ cup sour cream

Place cabbage in a large bowl with the water, cover, cook on HIGH for about 2 minutes or until cabbage is just wilted; drain. Combine bacon, onion and caraway seeds in a small bowl, cover, cook on HIGH for 3 minutes. Stir into cabbage with sour cream, cover, cook on MEDIUM for about 2 minutes or until heated through.

Serves 4.

CELERY WITH ORANGE SESAME GLAZE

Recipe unsuitable to freeze.

1 tablespoon oil
1 teaspoon sesame oil
4 sticks celery, thinly sliced
2 tablespoons light soya sauce
1 tablespoon sugar
2 teaspoons grated orange rind
1 teaspoon cornflour
⅓ cup orange juice
1 tablespoon sesame seeds, toasted

Heat oils in a shallow dish on HIGH for 1 minute. Add celery, cook on HIGH for 2 minutes, stir occasionally. Stir in soya sauce, sugar, orange rind and blended cornflour and orange juice. Cook on HIGH for about 3 minutes or until mixture boils and thickens. Sprinkle with sesame seeds before serving.

Serves 4.

PUMPKIN AND SPINACH ROLLS

Recipe unsuitable to freeze.

2 medium potatoes, chopped
200g pumpkin, chopped
15g butter
½ cup stale breadcrumbs
1 tablespoon chopped fresh chives
pinch nutmeg
4 large spinach (silverbeet) leaves

Combine potato and pumpkin in a bowl, cover, cook on HIGH for about 10 minutes or until tender. Stir in butter, breadcrumbs, chives and nutmeg; mash until smooth, cool the mixture.

Remove stems from spinach leaves, place flat in a shallow dish, cover, cook on HIGH for about 2 minutes or until just wilted; cool. Spread each spinach leaf with a quarter of the potato-pumpkin mixture, roll up.

Place seam side down in a single layer in a shallow dish, cover, cook on HIGH for about 3 minutes or until heated through; stand rolls for 2 minutes before serving.

Serves 4.

Clockwise from top: Celery with Orange Sesame Glaze; Creamy Caraway Cabbage; Pumpkin and Spinach Rolls.

China: Sasaki from Dansab

FENNEL WITH TOMATOES AND BASIL

Recipe unsuitable to freeze.

1 medium fennel bulb, chopped
1 medium onion, chopped
1 clove garlic, crushed
30g butter
310g can Tomato Supreme
½ cup dry white wine
2 tablespoons chopped fresh basil

Combine fennel, onion, garlic and butter in a large shallow dish, cover, cook on HIGH for 5 minutes, stir occasionally. Add Tomato Supreme and wine, cover, cook on HIGH for 12 minutes. Stir in basil just before serving.

Serves 4.

BACON AND CHEESE POTATOES

Recipe unsuitable to freeze.

750g baby new potatoes
¼ cup water
¼ cup grated parmesan cheese
2 bacon rashers, finely chopped
¼ cup cream
1 clove garlic, crushed
1 tablespoon chopped fresh parsley

Combine potatoes and water in a large shallow dish, cover, cook on HIGH for about 10 minutes or until potatoes are tender, drain. Stir in cheese, bacon, cream and garlic, cover, cook on HIGH for 2 minutes. Sprinkle with parsley just before serving.

Serves 4.

Top: Fennel with Tomatoes and Basil; bottom: Bacon and Cheese Potatoes.

Bowls: The Bay Tree; tiles: Pazotti

VEGETABLES
CONTINUED ON P.67

Our kitchen-tested tips and hints will help you to speed up all sorts of procedures when using the microwave oven.

HINTS

CHOCOLATE

Chocolate melts superbly in the microwave oven, but be careful of the timing as it will burn easily. Try these delicious ideas:

▲
To melt chocolate, place chocolate pieces on a plate in a single layer, cook on HIGH for about 1 minute for 100g, 2 minutes for 200g, etc. Stir until smooth. The chocolate retains its shape in the oven, but will spread when stirred.

To make a quick Chocolate Mint Sauce, combine 16 chocolate mint creams, ⅓ cup chocolate topping and ⅓ cup cream in a bowl, cook on HIGH for about 2 minutes, stir sauce until smooth.

For quick Choc-Mint Icing ▶ on patty cakes, place a chocolate after-dinner mint on each of 6 cakes, arrange cakes evenly on a large plate or around turntable, cook on HIGH for about 45 seconds or until chocolate is soft. Gently spread chocolate evenly over patty cakes.

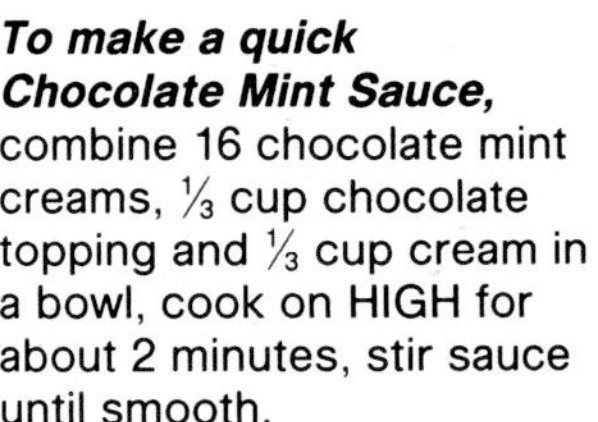

To make a quick Sour Cream Frosting, melt ½ cup of Choc Bits in a bowl on HIGH for about 1 minute, then add ½ cup of sour cream; whisk until mixture is smooth.

To make a quick piping bag to decorate cakes, slices or biscuits, etc, place 100g chopped chocolate in the corner of an oven bag, cook on HIGH for about 2 minutes or until chocolate is melted; press bag occasionally to ensure chocolate is melting evenly. Snip a small corner from bag and use as a piping bag.
▼

BREAD & ROLLS

▲
For hot dogs cooked in their rolls, place a scored frankfurt in a buttered roll and wrap in absorbent paper. Cook on HIGH for about 30 seconds.

To make croutons, melt 30g butter in a shallow dish, add 2 cups cubed bread, cook on HIGH for about 5 minutes or until bread is crisp and golden brown; stir occasionally.

To warm bread rolls or croissants, wrap each in absorbent paper, heat on HIGH for about 15 seconds for each roll or croissant.

DID YOU KNOW...?

. . . ***about a quick way*** to open mussels and oysters: place 6 to 8 around the edge of a plate or on the turntable, cook on HIGH for about 30 seconds to a minute; discard any unopened shells left after this cooking time.

HINTS

DRYING

To dry fresh bread crumbs, spread 2 cups crumbs out on absorbent paper, cook on HIGH for about 3 minutes; stir crumbs during cooking time.

To dry fresh herbs, wash and dry herbs well, place in a single layer between pieces of absorbent paper, cook on HIGH for about 3 minutes or until dry; cool to room temperature before storing in an airtight container. The time taken will depend on the water content of the fresh herbs. ▶

WARMING, SOFTENING & MELTING

Remove the last of the cream from the carton by heating on HIGH for about 15 seconds.

Soften too-hard ice-cream by heating on LOW for about 20 seconds at a time or until easier to scoop.

To warm brandy and spirits for flaming, pour into a jug, cook on HIGH for about 30 seconds, ignite carefully, pour over food.

Warm honey or golden syrup in an uncovered jar for accurate, easier measuring or serving by heating on HIGH for about 30 seconds.

Warm citrus fruit on HIGH for about 20 seconds to obtain more juice; stand for a few minutes before squeezing the fruit.

Crystallised honey can be liquefied in the jar, without the lid, by cooking on HIGH for about 30 seconds, depending on the quantity.

To warm jam for a quick glaze, heat a small amount in a bowl on HIGH for about 30 seconds; strain if necessary while hot.

To soften cream cheese and butter for beating, remove the wrapper, place in a bowl, heat on LOW for about 20 seconds.

Bring cheese to room temperature by heating on MEDIUM for about 20 seconds. This is good for camembert or brie which should not be eaten cold.

DID YOU KNOW...?

... ***how to heat serving plates:*** place a piece of damp paper towel between each plate in a stack, heat on HIGH for about 2 minutes.

... ***to heat hand towels:*** dampen towels and wring out well, heat on HIGH for about 1 minute.

... ***ring-shaped dishes*** or moulds are best for cooking cakes and many other recipes in the oven; they ensure even cooking. To improvise, place a glass in the centre of a round dish. ▼

FRUIT & VEGETABLES

Always pierce the skin on whole vegetables or fruit before cooking in the oven.

Cover vegetables before cooking in the oven to minimise dehydration and decrease cooking. Only a little water has to be added before cooking, depending on the vegetable. Often, washed and well-drained vegetables have enough water on them for cooking.

To make pumpkin easier to cut and peel, heat a piece of pumpkin on HIGH for about 2 minutes.

Frozen vegetables can be ▶ cooked in the bag in which they are purchased; always pierce the bag in several places before cooking.

To reconstitute dried fruit (apricots, apples, etc): place 1 cup of fruit in a bowl, cover with cold water, cook on HIGH for about 6 minutes; stand, covered, for 5 minutes before using.

To plump raisins or prunes, add 1 tablespoon of juice or water to 1 cup of fruit in a bowl (follow individual recipes), cover, cook on HIGH for about 30 seconds; stand 3 minutes.

DID YOU KNOW...?

... ***you can continue to cook*** an underdone boiled egg by cutting off the top and replacing it, then cooking the egg on HIGH for only a few seconds.

... ***that 1 cup of cold water*** takes about 2½ minutes to boil on HIGH.

... ***to use 2 patty cases*** together for patty cakes and muffins; this helps to absorb moisture during cooking and cooling.

... ***you should whisk sauces*** several times during cooking; if not whisked, the sauce will form lumps at the bottom of the dish.

... ***it is wise*** to use only plastic ware that has been marked microwave safe.

SOAKING DRIED FOOD

Speed the time needed for soaking peas, beans and lentils, etc, this way:

To soak burghul (cracked wheat), place ½ cup burghul in a bowl, cover with cold water, cover, cook on HIGH for 5 minutes, stand 5 minutes, drain well; dry on absorbent paper or a tea towel before using.

For chick peas, place 250g in a large bowl with 4 cups of cold water, cover, cook on HIGH for about 9 minutes or until boiling. Stand for 1 hour before using. (***For lentils,*** cook covered for about 4 minutes. ***Kidney beans and haricot beans,*** cook covered for about 6 minutes.)

TOASTING

It is very convenient and economical to "toast" in the microwave oven. Here are instructions for sesame seeds, almonds and coconut:

Sesame seeds: melt a teaspoon of butter in a pie plate, stir in ¼ cup sesame seeds, cook on HIGH for about 3 minutes or until seeds are lightly browned; stir the seeds occasionally during cooking time. ▶

Almonds: place 1 cup almonds in a dish in a single layer, cook on HIGH for about 5 minutes or until lightly browned; stir the almonds occasionally during cooking. ▶

◀ ***Coconut:*** place 1 cup coconut in an oven bag, cook on HIGH for about 4 minutes; shake bag several times during cooking.

FOR EASIER COOKING

To clarify butter, melt 125g butter in a bowl on LOW for about 5 minutes or until foaming. Skim off foam and discard, stand butter for 4 minutes then pour or spoon off clear liquid; this is the clarified butter.

To par-cook sausages, place 1kg thick sausages in a single layer in a large shallow dish with 2 cups of cold water, cook on HIGH for about 10 minutes, turning sausages halfway through cooking time.

Cook pappadams by placing 4 large pappadams in a single layer around the edge of a plate or turntable, cook on HIGH for about 4 minutes, turning after 2 minutes (4 small pappadams will take about 1 minute). ▶

Cook a quick egg for breakfast by breaking an egg into an ordinary tea cup (greasing is not necessary). Pierce yolk with a fork or skewer, cook on HIGH for about 30 seconds.

HINTS

DID YOU KNOW...?

▲ . . . ***to shield corners*** of square or rectangular containers with foil to prevent over-cooking, especially with cakes, meat loaves, slices, etc. Also use foil to cover chicken wings and drumstick bones to prevent overcooking. ▶

. . . ***it is best to use*** large shallow dishes where possible; this means the food is spread out to make the cooking more even.

Be careful of steam *when removing plastic covering from dishes; do this away from you, as shown.* ▶

We used a microwave-safe *polyethylene plastic food wrap to cover foods. It is not necessary to pierce the plastic or leave a vent for steam to escape.*

. . . ***gold or silver trimmed plates*** can cause "arcing" in the oven Remove them if this happens.

Picture shows the muffin dish *ideal for microwave use.* ▼

◀ ***Picture shows the four different ring dishes*** *used throughout this book.*

Remember to measure inside top of all dishes *to comply with our recipes.*

REVIVAL TECHNIQUES

To soften a packet of tortillas, split packet and heat on HIGH for about 40 seconds.

To crispen slightly stale cookies, potato crisps and breakfast cereals, spread out in a single layer on absorbent paper, cook on HIGH for about 15 seconds.

To soften lumpy brown sugar, place in a bowl with a thick slice of apple on top, cover, cook on HIGH for about 30 seconds; stand 5 minutes before using the sugar.

To reheat a cooked roast, or whole plum pudding, place the food in an oven bag, secure the opening loosely and cook on HIGH until food is heated.

To soften lumpy icing sugar, place in a bowl, cover, cook on HIGH for about 15 seconds; cool before using the sugar.

Table: Freedom Furniture

Sweet and Sour Cabbage

SWEET AND SOUR CABBAGE

Recipe unsuitable to freeze.

6 bacon rashers, chopped
1 medium onion, chopped
1 teaspoon grated orange rind
2 tablespoons orange juice
2 tablespoons dry sherry
2 teaspoons sugar
2 tablespoons tomato sauce
2 teaspoons light soya sauce
2 teaspoons cornflour
2 tablespoons water
5 cups finely shredded cabbage (about ¼ large cabbage)

Place bacon in a shallow dish, cook on HIGH for 3 minutes, drain; cook on HIGH for about 3 minutes or until bacon is crisp, drain on absorbent paper.

Combine onion, orange rind and juice, sherry, sugar and sauces in a bowl, cover, cook on HIGH for 3 minutes. Stir in blended cornflour and water, cook on HIGH for about 1 minute or until mixture boils and thickens. Place cabbage in a large shallow dish, add onion mixture, cover, cook on HIGH for about 3 minutes or until tender, sprinkle with bacon.

Serves 4.

GOLDEN PUMPKINS WITH CREAMY VEGETABLE MIX

Recipe unsuitable to freeze.

2 small golden nugget pumpkins
4 tablespoons water
3 medium potatoes
½ cup fresh or frozen green peas
½ cup fresh or frozen corn kernels
¼ cup grated tasty cheese
ground nutmeg
SAUCE
2 teaspoons butter
2 teaspoons plain flour
¾ cup milk
1 small chicken stock cube, crumbled

Cut pumpkins in half, remove seeds, place pumpkin halves, cut side up, on a flat dish. Place 1 tablespoon of water into each half, cover halves with plastic wrap, cook on HIGH for about 6 minutes or until pumpkins are just tender.

Cut potatoes into 1cm cubes, place in a shallow dish, cover with hot water, cover, cook on HIGH for about 10 minutes or until potatoes are tender, stir occasionally; drain.

Combine peas and corn in bowl, sprinkle with about a tablespoon of water, cover, cook on HIGH for about 5 minutes or until tender; drain.

Combine vegetables and sauce in bowl, mix well, spoon into each pumpkin shell, top with cheese, sprinkle with nutmeg. Cook on HIGH for about 2 minutes or until filling is hot and cheese melted.

Sauce: Melt butter in a bowl on HIGH for 15 seconds, stir in flour then milk and stock cube. Cook on HIGH for about 3 minutes or until sauce boils and thickens, stir occasionally.

Serves 4.

CRUNCHY SNOW PEA AND CARROT STIR-FRY

Recipe unsuitable to freeze.

30g butter
1 teaspoon grated fresh ginger
1 clove garlic, crushed
1 small fresh red chilli, chopped
2 medium carrots
250g snow peas
1 tablespoon dry sherry
1 tablespoon light soya sauce

Combine butter, ginger, garlic and chilli in a large bowl, cover, cook on HIGH for 1 minute. Cut carrots into thin strips, add to bowl, cover, cook on HIGH for 2 minutes. Add snow peas, sherry and soya sauce, cover, cook on HIGH for 2 minutes.

Serves 4.

Dish: Pillivuyt from Zuhause

Dishes: Mikasa; tiles: Pazotti

CHEESE AND HERB TOMATOES

Recipe unsuitable to freeze.

500g tomatoes
15g butter
⅓ cup packaged breadcrumbs
2 tablespoons chopped fresh parsley
½ teaspoon dried basil leaves
½ teaspoon dried oregano leaves
⅓ cup coarsely grated fresh parmesan cheese

Cut tomatoes into 1cm thick slices, place slices slightly overlapping in a large shallow dish. Melt butter in a small bowl on HIGH for 15 seconds, stir in breadcrumbs and herbs, cook on HIGH for 2 minutes, stir occasionally. Stir in cheese, sprinkle mixture evenly over tomatoes, cook on HIGH for about 4 minutes or until tomatoes are heated through.

Serves 4.

ABOVE: Top: Crunchy Snow Pea and Carrot Stir-Fry; bottom: Golden Pumpkins with Creamy Vegetable Mix. LEFT: Cheese and Herb Tomatoes.

ORANGE HONEY BEETROOT

Recipe unsuitable to freeze.

750g beetroot
30g butter
1 teaspoon grated orange rind
2 tablespoons orange juice
1 tablespoon honey

Peel beetroot, cut into 1cm strips. Combine beetroot with butter and rind in a large shallow dish, cover, cook on HIGH for 4 minutes; stir halfway through cooking. Stir in orange juice and honey, cover, cook on HIGH for about 4 minutes or until tender.

Serves 4.

CHEESY SPINACH IN POTATO CASES

Recipe unsuitable to freeze.

4 medium potatoes
oil
1 bunch English spinach (40 leaves)
15g butter
1 small onion, finely chopped
¾ cup stale breadcrumbs
½ cup sour cream
1 cup grated tasty cheese
1 egg, separated
1 teaspoon ground nutmeg
2 tablespoons coarsely grated fresh parmesan cheese

Pierce unpeeled potatoes in several places with fork, rub potatoes with oil, place on a flat dish, cook on HIGH for about 10 minutes or until just tender; stand 5 minutes. Place spinach in a large bowl, cover, cook on HIGH for 3 minutes; squeeze dry. Chop or process spinach until finely chopped.

Combine butter and onion in a bowl, cook on HIGH for 3 minutes, stir in breadcrumbs, sour cream and tasty cheese, cook on HIGH for 2 minutes, stir occasionally.

Cut tops from potatoes, carefully scoop out potato flesh, do not break the outside skin. Mash three-quarters cup of the potato, place in a bowl, stir in spinach, egg yolk and nutmeg. Beat egg white until soft peaks form, fold through spinach mixture, spoon into potatoes, sprinkle with parmesan cheese. Cook on HIGH for about 3 minutes or until heated through.

Serves 4.

China: Sasaki from Dansab

Dish: Pillivuyt from Zuhause

China: The Bay Tree; tiles: Country Floors

MINTED LEMON PARSNIPS

Recipe unsuitable to freeze.

500g parsnips, thinly sliced
¼ cup sugar
1 teaspoon grated lemon rind
2 tablespoons lemon juice
1 tablespoon chopped fresh mint

Place parsnips in a large shallow dish, cover with boiling water, cover, cook on HIGH for about 8 minutes or until parsnips are tender, drain.

Combine sugar, lemon rind and juice in a small bowl. Cook on HIGH for about 6 minutes, stir occasionally. Pour sugar syrup over parsnips and cook on HIGH for about 2 minutes or until heated through. Sprinkle with mint just before serving.

Serves 4.

ZUCCHINI WITH ORANGE RICE

You will need to cook about 1 tablespoon brown rice for this recipe. Recipe unsuitable to freeze.

4 medium zucchini
¼ cup cooked brown rice
1 green shallot, chopped
2 tablespoons grated tasty cheese
1 tablespoon chopped fresh oregano
2 teaspoons grated orange rind
1 tablespoon cream

Halve zucchini lengthways, place in a single layer in a shallow dish, cover, cook on HIGH for about 3 minutes or until zucchini are just tender, cool.

Scoop out flesh from zucchini, leaving shells intact; return shells to dish. Combine zucchini flesh, rice, shallot, cheese, oregano, orange rind and cream in a bowl, mix well. Spoon rice mixture into zucchini shells, cook on HIGH for 3 minutes or until hot.

Serves 4.

ABOVE LEFT: Left: Minted Lemon Parsnips; right: Orange Honey Beetroot. BELOW, FAR LEFT: Cheesy Spinach in Potato Cases. BELOW, LEFT: Zucchini with Orange Rice.

Dish: The Bay Tree; table: Freedom Furniture

PUMPKIN ZUCCHINI LOAF

Recipe unsuitable to freeze

350g pumpkin, chopped
310g can butter beans, drained
15g butter
1 medium onion, finely chopped
2 bacon rashers, chopped
2 teaspoons curry powder
3 small zucchini, grated
1 cup grated tasty cheese
3 eggs, lightly beaten
1 cup stale breadcrumbs
SWEET HERB SAUCE
1 tablespoon sugar
⅔ cup water
2 tablespoons white vinegar
2 teaspoons cornflour
1 tablespoon chopped fresh mint
1 tablespoon chopped fresh parsley
2 teaspoons chopped fresh dill
2 teaspoons chopped fresh chives

Grease a 12cm x 22cm loaf dish, line base with paper, grease paper. Place pumpkin in a large shallow dish, cover, cook on HIGH for about 8 minutes or until pumpkin is tender. Blend or process pumpkin and beans until smooth.

Combine onion, bacon, and curry powder in a bowl, cover, cook on HIGH for 4 minutes. Stir in pumpkin mixture, then remaining ingredients, pour into prepared dish, cover, cook on HIGH for about 18 minutes or until loaf feels firm. Stand loaf, covered, for 10 minutes before serving. Serve warm or cold with sauce.

Sweet Herb Sauce: Combine sugar and water in a bowl, cook on HIGH for 2 minutes, stir in blended vinegar and cornflour, cook on HIGH for about 1 minute or until sauce boils and thickens. Stir in herbs just before serving.

CAULIFLOWER WITH TOMATO AND PEPPER SAUCE

Cauliflower and sauce can be prepared separately for up to 2 days ahead. Recipe unsuitable to freeze.

½ medium cauliflower
30g butter
1 clove garlic, crushed
1 medium onion, chopped
1 tablespoon tomato paste
¼ cup tomato purée
1 medium green pepper
½ teaspoon dried tarragon leaves
1 tablespoon grated parmesan cheese
¼ teaspoon paprika

Cut cauliflower into flowerets. Combine butter, garlic and onion in a large shallow dish, cover, cook on HIGH for 3 minutes. Stir in tomato paste, tomato purée, pepper and tarragon, then cauliflower, cover, cook on HIGH for about 15 minutes or until cauliflower is tender. Top with cheese, sprinkle with paprika, cook on HIGH for 2 minutes.

Serves 4.

LAYERED TOMATO AND POTATO CASSEROLE

Recipe unsuitable to freeze.

30g butter
1 medium potato, sliced
4 medium tomatoes, peeled, sliced
90g butter, extra
1 clove garlic, crushed
CHEESY EGG TOPPING
½ cup stale wholemeal breadcrumbs
1 tablespoon grated parmesan cheese
2 tablespoons grated tasty cheese
¼ cup flaked almonds, toasted
2 hard-boiled eggs, chopped
2 green shallots, chopped

Melt butter in a shallow dish on HIGH for 30 seconds, add potato in a single layer, cover, cook on HIGH for about 3 minutes or until potato is tender. Top with half the tomatoes and half the topping mixture, repeat with remaining tomatoes and topping.

Combine extra butter and garlic in small bowl, cook on HIGH for 1 minute, drizzle over topping. Cook on HIGH for about 8 minutes or until mixture is heated through.

Cheesy Egg Topping: Combine all ingredients in a bowl; mix well.

Serves 4.

ABOVE: Pumpkin Zucchini Loaf.
RIGHT: Left: Layered Tomato and Potato Casserole; right: Cauliflower with Tomato and Pepper Sauce.

China: The Bay Tree; tiles: Pazotti

PORK

Tender cuts of pork taste delicious used in these new and attractive ways. For the best results, buy lean cuts of even size. Almost all the recipes are simple to make and are best when cooked and served immediately.

PORK AND MUSTARD STROGANOFF

Recipe unsuitable to freeze.

30g butter
1 small onion, thinly sliced
600g pork fillets, thinly sliced
200g baby mushrooms, sliced
2 tablespoons seeded mustard
1 small chicken stock cube, crumbled
¼ cup water
1 teaspoon cornflour
½ cup sour cream
2 tablespoons chopped fresh parsley

Combine butter and onion in a large shallow dish, cook on HIGH for 3 minutes. Add pork, cook on HIGH for about 5 minutes or until pork is tender; stir occasionally. Add mushrooms, mustard, stock cube, blended water and cornflour. Cook on HIGH for about 2 minutes or until mixture boils and thickens. Stir in sour cream and parsley; reheat, if necessary.

Serves 4.

BARBECUED PORK STIR-FRY

Recipe unsuitable to freeze.

375g barbecued pork
30g (about 10) Chinese dried mushrooms
1 tablespoon oil
1 teaspoon sesame oil
2 cloves garlic, crushed
4 green shallots, chopped
3 cups Chinese thin egg noodles
250g snow peas, halved
4 cups thinly sliced Chinese cabbage (about ½ large Chinese cabbage)
1 cup bean sprouts

Dish: Reflections Gift Boutique; cane cabinet: Keyhole Furniture

3 teaspoons cornflour
1 cup water
1 small chicken stock cube, crumbled
1 tablespoon light soya sauce
½ teaspoon ground cumin
½ teaspoon ground coriander

Slice pork thinly. Cover mushrooms with hot water, stand 20 minutes, drain, remove and discard stems, slice mushroom caps.

Combine oil, sesame oil, garlic and shallots in a large shallow dish, cook on HIGH for 1 minute. Add pork, mushrooms, noodles, snow peas, cabbage

and sprouts. Stir in blended cornflour and water, stock cube, soya sauce, cumin and coriander. Cook on HIGH for about 6 minutes or until sauce boils and thickens; stir occasionally.

Serves 4.

SHERRIED PORK SPARERIBS

Recipe unsuitable to freeze.

1kg pork spareribs
¼ cup dry sherry
2 tablespoons light soya sauce
2 tablespoons tomato sauce
2 tablespoons honey
2 tablespoons lemon juice
2 teaspoons grated fresh ginger
2 cloves garlic, crushed
2 teaspoons cornflour
1 tablespoon water

Remove rind and excess fat from ribs, cut ribs into 3cm lengths.

Combine sherry, sauces, honey, lemon juice, ginger and garlic in a large bowl, add pork; mix well. Cover, refrigerate for 2 hours or overnight.

Drain pork, reserve marinade. Place pork pieces on a rack in a single layer over a shallow dish. Cook on HIGH for about 14 minutes or until pork is tender; turn pork occasionally. Blend cornflour with water, add to reserved marinade in bowl, cook on HIGH for about 3 minutes or until mixture boils and thickens; stir occasionally. Serve over spareribs.

Serves 4.

ABOVE: Left: Barbecued Pork Stir-Fry; right: Sherried Pork Spareribs. LEFT: Pork and Mustard Stroganoff.

PORK WITH PRUNES AND APRICOTS

Recipe unsuitable to freeze.

⅓ cup chopped prunes
⅓ cup chopped dried apricots
¼ cup red currant jelly
½ cup dry white wine
1 chicken stock cube, crumbled
4 pork steaks (schnitzels)
15g butter
1 clove garlic, crushed
2 teaspoons cornflour
¼ cup water

Combine prunes, apricots, jelly, wine and stock cube in a bowl, cover, cook on HIGH for 1 minute; cool. Add steaks to prune and apricot mixture, cover, refrigerate several hours or overnight.

Combine butter and garlic in a large shallow dish, cook on HIGH for 1 minute. Remove steaks from marinade; reserve marinade. Add steaks to dish in a single layer, cook on HIGH for 6 minutes, turning steaks occasionally. Stir in reserved marinade and blended cornflour and water, cook on HIGH for about 3 minutes or until mixture boils and thickens; stir occasionally.

Serves 4.

CURRIED PORK WITH MANGO

Recipe unsuitable to freeze.

1 tablespoon oil
1 medium green pepper, sliced
1 medium onion, sliced
1 clove garlic, crushed
1 small fresh red chilli, chopped
¼ teaspoon ground cardamom
1 teaspoon garam masala
¼ teaspoon ground coriander
750g pork fillets, thinly sliced
1 tablespoon tomato paste
2 teaspoons cornflour
1 small beef stock cube, crumbled
¼ cup water
2 large mangoes, sliced

Combine oil, pepper, onion, garlic, chilli and spices in a large shallow dish, cover, cook on HIGH for 3 minutes. Add pork and tomato paste, cover, cook on HIGH for about 12 minutes or until pork is tender; stir occasionally. Stir in cornflour and stock cube blended with the water, cook on HIGH for about 2 minutes or until mixture boils and thickens. Serve with mangoes.

Serves 4.

Plate: Reflections Gift Boutique; cane cabinet: Keyhole Furniture

SPICY PORK WITH STIR-FRIED VEGETABLES

Recipe unsuitable to freeze.

¼ cup light soya sauce
1 tablespoon hoisin sauce
1 tablespoon sweet chilli sauce
1 tablespoon honey
1 clove garlic, crushed
1 teaspoon grated fresh ginger
500g pork fillets, thinly sliced
250g broccoli
425g can baby corn, drained
1 tablespoon oil
1 medium red pepper, chopped
1 medium onion, quartered
1 stick celery, sliced
3 teaspoons cornflour
1 tablespoon water

Combine sauces, honey, garlic, ginger and pork in a bowl; mix well, cover, refrigerate several hours or overnight.

Cut broccoli into flowerets, cut corn into quarters lengthways. Place oil in a shallow dish, heat on HIGH for 1 minute. Add broccoli and corn to dish with remaining vegetables, cook on HIGH for 4 minutes, stir occasionally.

Stir in pork and marinade, cook on HIGH for 7 minutes; stir occasionally. Stir in blended cornflour and water, cook on HIGH for about 2 minutes or until mixture boils and thickens.

Serves 4.

ABOVE: Spicy Pork with Stir-Fried Vegetables. LEFT: Top: Curried Pork with Mango; bottom: Pork with Prunes and Apricots.

SPICY PORK AND SAUSAGE HOT POT

Recipe can be made up to 2 days ahead. Recipe unsuitable to freeze.

750g pork butterfly steaks
1 tablespoon oil
1 clove garlic, chopped
1 medium onion, chopped
¼ teaspoon ground cloves
¼ cup tomato paste
2 teaspoons paprika
2 chorizo sausages, chopped
310g can butter beans, drained, rinsed
250g baby mushrooms, chopped
1 medium green pepper, chopped
½ teaspoon cayenne pepper
½ teaspoon dried oregano leaves
1 cup tomato purée
1 teaspoon sugar
½ cup grated parmesan cheese

Cut pork into 3cm cubes. Combine pork, oil, garlic, onion and cloves in a large shallow dish, cover, cook on HIGH for 3 minutes, stir halfway through cooking time.

Stir in tomato paste, paprika, sausages, beans, mushrooms, pepper, cayenne, oregano, purée and sugar, cover, cook on HIGH for about 10 minutes or until pork is tender; stir halfway through cooking time. Sprinkle with cheese, cook on HIGH for about 2 minutes or until cheese is melted.

Serves 4.

Dishes: Reflections Gift Boutique

Table: Keyhole Furniture

PORK AND KUMARA CASSEROLE

Recipe unsuitable to freeze.

750g pork steaks (schnitzels)
1 teaspoon grated fresh ginger
1 medium onion, quartered
1 medium kumara, chopped
1 small fresh red chilli, chopped
2 tablespoons oyster sauce
2 tablespoons barbecue satay-style sauce
2 tablespoons dark soya sauce
2 teaspoons cornflour
½ cup water
1 teaspoon chopped fresh coriander
1 teaspoon chopped fresh mint

Cut pork into 6cm strips. Combine pork and ginger in a large shallow dish, cover, cook on HIGH for 3 minutes. Stir in onion, kumara, chilli, sauces and blended cornflour and water, cover, cook on HIGH for about 7 minutes or

until pork is tender; stir occasionally. Sprinkle with coriander and mint before serving.

Serves 4.

PORK CORDON BLEU

Recipe unsuitable to freeze.

4 pork steaks (schnitzels)
8 slices ham
2 cups grated tasty cheese
½ teaspoon dried oregano leaves
plain flour
1 egg, lightly beaten
2 cups stale breadcrumbs
1 teaspoon paprika
60g butter, melted

Spread plastic wrap over steaks, pound steaks out thinly. Cover each steak with 2 slices of ham, top with combined cheese and oregano. Fold pork in half, toss in flour, shake off excess flour. Dip pork in egg, then combined breadcrumbs and paprika. Brush pork with butter, cover, refrigerate for 30 minutes.

Heat a browning dish, place pork on browning dish in a single layer, brown pork on both sides, then cook on HIGH for about 6 minutes or until tender.

Serves 4.

PORK WITH CREAMY APPLE AND MUSHROOM SAUCE

Recipe unsuitable to freeze.

30g butter
4 green shallots, sliced
4 pork steaks (schnitzels)
100g baby mushrooms, sliced
2 teaspoons cornflour
¼ cup cream
½ cup clear apple juice
½ cup water
1 small beef stock cube, crumbled

Melt butter in a large shallow dish, add shallots and pork in a single layer, cover, cook on HIGH for about 8 minutes or until pork is almost tender. Turn steaks once during cooking. Stir in mushrooms, cover, cook on HIGH for 2 minutes.

Blend cornflour with cream, stir in juice, water and stock cube, add to pork mixture, cover, cook on HIGH for about 2 minutes or until mixture boils and thickens; stir occasionally.

Serves 4.

ABOVE: Left: Pork Cordon Bleu; right: Pork with Creamy Apple and Mushroom Sauce. LEFT: Top: Pork and Kumara Casserole; bottom: Spicy Pork and Sausage Hot Pot.

HONEY AND SESAME PORK MEDALLIONS

Recipe unsuitable to freeze.

4 pork medallions
2 tablespoons hoisin sauce
1 tablespoon light soya sauce
1 tablespoon honey
pinch five spice powder
½ teaspoon sesame oil
1 tablespoon sesame seeds
SHERRY SAUCE
1½ teaspoons cornflour
2 tablespoons dry sherry
2 tablespoons hoisin sauce
1 tablespoon honey

Place pork in a single layer in a large shallow dish, pour over combined sauces, honey, five spice powder and sesame oil.

Place pork in a single layer on a rack, cook on HIGH for about 8 minutes or until tender, turning occasionally. Brush with any remaining honey mixture during cooking. Sprinkle with sesame seeds and serve with sauce.

Sherry Sauce: Blend cornflour with sherry in small bowl, stir in sauce and honey, cook on HIGH for about 1 minute or until sauce boils and thickens.

Serves 4.

Plates and fork: Mikasa; background: Wilson Fabrics

SWEET 'N' SPICY PORK

Recipe unsuitable to freeze.

30g butter
1 clove garlic, crushed
1 medium onion, chopped
1 small red pepper, sliced
1 small green pepper, sliced
1 teaspoon turmeric
1 teaspoon garam masala
½ teaspoon ground cumin
½ teaspoon ground ginger
500g pork fillets, sliced
440g can tomato soup
1 tablespoon mango chutney

Combine butter, garlic, onion, peppers, turmeric, garam masala, cumin and ginger in large bowl, cover, cook on HIGH for 5 minutes. Add pork, undiluted soup and chutney, cover, cook on HIGH for about 10 minutes or until pork is tender; stir occasionally.

Serves 4.

Plates: Made in Japan

CURRIED HAM AND CORN PATTIES

Patties can be prepared up to a day before cooking or frozen for up to 1 month. Thaw overnight in refrigerator.

2 medium potatoes, thinly sliced
2 tablespoons water
30g butter
1 small onion, chopped
1 clove garlic, crushed
185g ham, finely chopped
1 tablespoon curry powder
130g can creamed corn
½ cup stale breadcrumbs
2 tablespoons chopped fresh parsley
1 egg, lightly beaten
2 tablespoons milk
½ cup packaged breadcrumbs
¼ cup grated parmesan cheese
1 tablespoon chopped fresh parsley, extra

Rinse potatoes under cold water; do not dry. Place potatoes in a single layer in a large shallow dish, sprinkle with the water, cover, cook on HIGH for about 8 minutes or until tender. Drain potatoes, mash until smooth.

Combine butter, onion, garlic, ham and curry powder in a large bowl, cover, cook on HIGH for 3 minutes. Stir in corn, potatoes, stale breadcrumbs and parsley. Shape mixture into 6 patties, dip in combined egg and milk, then toss in combined packaged breadcrumbs, cheese and extra parsley.

Place a sheet of baking paper on a flat dish, place patties around the edge of the dish, cook on HIGH for 4 minutes, turn patties, cook on HIGH for another 4 minutes.

Makes 6.

LEFT: Sweet 'n' Spicy Pork. ABOVE: Left: Honey and Sesame Pork Medallions; right: Curried Ham and Corn Patties.

LAMB

As with all meat, it is best to choose cuts of lamb that are as similar in size as possible to allow for even cooking. Buy lean lamb; trim any fat, if necessary.

China: Mikasa; fork: Limoges

China: Limoges; background: Wilson Fabrics

CHEESY LAMB FILLETS WITH QUICK TOMATO SAUCE

Recipe unsuitable to freeze.

8 lamb fillets
125g ricotta cheese
2 tablespoons grated parmesan cheese
1 tablespoon Worcestershire sauce
QUICK TOMATO SAUCE
310g can Tomato Supreme
1 tablespoon tomato paste
2 tablespoons chopped fresh parsley

Trim excess fat and sinew from lamb fillets, cover with plastic wrap, pound with meat mallet until thin. Spread fillets with combined ricotta and parmesan cheese, fold in half, secure with toothpicks. Brush fillets with Worcestershire sauce.

Place on a rack in single layer with folded end facing to the outside of the rack. Place rack into a large shallow dish, cook on HIGH for about 4 minutes or until lamb is just tender, turn once during cooking. Serve with tomato sauce.

Quick Tomato Sauce: Combine all ingredients in a bowl, cook on HIGH for about 2 minutes or until mixture boils.

Serves 4.

APRICOT LAMB WITH HONEY SAUCE

Ask the butcher to remove the bone from the leg of lamb for you. Recipe unsuitable to freeze.

1½kg leg of lamb, boned
APRICOT FILLING
¼ cup buckwheat
⅓ cup chopped dried apricots
2 green shallots, chopped
2 tablespoons pine nuts
1½ tablespoons fruit chutney

LEFT: Top: Apricot Lamb with Honey Sauce; bottom: Lamb Fillets with Vegetable Julienne. FAR LEFT: Cheesy Lamb Fillets with Quick Tomato Sauce.

HONEY SAUCE
⅓ cup honey
1½ tablespoons light soya sauce
⅓ cup orange juice
2 teaspoons grated fresh ginger
2 teaspoons cornflour
2 tablespoons water

Open the lamb out flat, place fat-side down on bench, press filling over lamb, bring edges together, tie lamb firmly with string.

Place lamb seam-side down on a rack, place over a shallow dish, cook on HIGH for 10 minutes. Turn lamb, cook on MEDIUM HIGH for 10 minutes. Turn lamb, cook on MEDIUM HIGH for about 10 minutes or until lamb is cooked as desired. Cover lamb with foil, stand 5 minutes while preparing sauce. Serve lamb with honey sauce.

Apricot Filling: Cover buckwheat with cold water, stand 20 minutes, drain well. Combine buckwheat, apricots, shallots, pine nuts and chutney in a bowl; mix well.

Honey Sauce: Combine honey, soya sauce, orange juice and ginger in a bowl, stir in blended cornflour and water, cook on HIGH for about 3 minutes or until mixture boils and thickens; stir occasionally.

Serves 6.

LAMB FILLETS WITH VEGETABLE JULIENNE

Recipe unsuitable to freeze.

8 lamb fillets
1 clove garlic, crushed
1 tablespoon oil
2 teaspoons light soya sauce
2 teaspoons oil, extra
1 medium carrot
1 medium leek
1 medium zucchini
60g butter
pinch five spice powder
2 teaspoons cornflour
1 tablespoon dry sherry
½ cup water
½ small chicken stock cube, crumbled

Combine lamb, garlic, oil and soya sauce in a bowl, cover, marinate several hours or overnight.

Preheat a browning dish on HIGH, add half the extra oil and half the lamb, turn when browned, remove lamb. Reheat dish, repeat with remaining oil and lamb.

Place all lamb on browning dish, cook on HIGH for 2 minutes or until lamb is cooked as desired. Remove lamb, reserve liquid.

Slice vegetables thinly, cut into thin strips. Combine butter with carrot and leek in a large shallow dish, cover, cook on HIGH for 3 minutes. Add zucchini and five spice powder, cover, cook on HIGH for 2 minutes. Blend cornflour with sherry, water, stock cube and reserved liquid in bowl, cook on HIGH for about 2 minutes or until mixture boils and thickens. Place vegetables on serving plate, top with sliced lamb, then sauce.

Serves 4.

LAMB

PISTACHIO HONEYED LAMB

Recipe unsuitable to freeze.

½ teaspoon dried mixed herbs
¼ cup barbecue sauce
1 tablespoon honey
1 clove garlic, crushed
¾ cup pistachio nuts, shelled, chopped
2 racks lamb (6 cutlets in each)

Combine herbs, sauce, honey and garlic in a small bowl, brush evenly over lamb. Stand racks upright in a shallow dish. Cook on MEDIUM for 10 minutes, turn racks, cook on HIGH for a further 5 minutes.

Press nuts evenly onto lamb, cook on HIGH for about 5 more minutes or until lamb is tender.

Serves 4.

GARLIC AND GINGER LAMB

Use a leg of lamb or thick leg chops for this recipe. Recipe can be frozen for up to 2 months.

750g lean lamb
2 tablespoons light soya sauce
1 teaspoon grated fresh ginger
2 cloves garlic, crushed
3 green shallots, chopped
½ teaspoon five spice powder
¼ cup dry sherry
1 tablespoon oil
1 tablespoon cornflour
1 small chicken stock cube, crumbled
¼ cup water

Trim lamb, cut into bite-sized pieces. Combine lamb, soya sauce, ginger, garlic, shallots, five spice powder and sherry in a bowl; cover, refrigerate several hours or overnight.

Heat oil in a large shallow dish, add lamb mixture, cover, cook on HIGH for about 10 minutes or until lamb is just tender; stir occasionally. Blend cornflour, stock cube and water together in a bowl, stir into lamb mixture, cook on HIGH for about 2 minutes or until mixture boils and thickens.

Serves 4.

China: Villeroy & Boch; tiles: Pazotti

ABOVE RIGHT: Pistachio Honeyed Lamb. FAR RIGHT: From top: Curried Lamb with Coconut Cream; Garlic and Ginger Lamb; Lamb with Mango.

LAMB WITH MANGO

Recipe unsuitable to freeze.

2 tablespoons fruit chutney
1 teaspoon curry powder
1 clove garlic, crushed
2 tablespoons orange juice
2 teaspoons honey
8 lamb chump chops
3 teaspoons cornflour
1 tablespoon water
1 mango, sliced

Combine chutney, curry powder, garlic, orange juice, honey and chops in a large bowl, mix well, stand 10 minutes. Place 4 chops on a rack over a dish, cook on HIGH for about 4 minutes or until tender; turn once during cooking. Remove chops, repeat with remaining chops; reserve any liquid.

Place 1 cup of the reserved liquid into a bowl with blended cornflour and water, cook on HIGH for about 2 minutes or until mixture boils and thickens. Place mango and chops on serving plate, top with sauce, cover, reheat on HIGH for about 1 minute.

Serves 4.

CURRIED LAMB WITH COCONUT CREAM

Curry can be made 3 days ahead. Recipe unsuitable to freeze.

30g butter
1 medium onion, sliced
750g boneless chopped lamb
1 cup hot water

70g packet Dutch Curry and Rice Soup
½ teaspoon ground cumin
½ teaspoon chilli powder
1 teaspoon turmeric
2 tablespoons coconut
2 tablespoons sultanas
¼ cup coconut cream
2 teaspoons chopped fresh coriander

Combine butter and onion in a large shallow dish, cover, cook on HIGH for 3 minutes. Add lamb, water, dry soup mix, cumin, chilli, turmeric, coconut and sultanas. Cover, cook on HIGH for 5 minutes, then on MEDIUM for about 15 minutes or until tender. Add coconut cream, sprinkle with coriander.

Serves 4.

Dishes: Made in Japan

LEMON AND APRICOT RACKS OF LAMB

Recipe unsuitable to freeze.

2 racks of lamb (6 cutlets in each)
1 tablespoon honey
1 tablespoon lemon juice
1 tablespoon chopped fresh mint
2 teaspoons light soya sauce
LEMON AND APRICOT SEASONING
30g butter
1 medium onion, finely chopped
2 bacon rashers, chopped
⅓ cup chopped dried apricots
1 tablespoon chopped fresh mint
1 teaspoon grated lemon rind
1 cup stale white breadcrumbs
1 egg yolk

Interlock racks of lamb on a flat dish, fill centre with seasoning. Brush racks all over with combined honey, lemon juice, mint and soya sauce, cook on HIGH for about 16 minutes or until lamb is almost cooked; brush occasionally with honey mixture during cooking. Cover lamb with foil, stand 10 minutes before serving.

Lemon and Apricot Seasoning: Combine butter, onion, bacon and apricots in a bowl, cook on HIGH for 3 minutes. Stir in remaining ingredients.

Serves 4.

OLD-FASHIONED LAMB AND VEGETABLE CASSEROLE

Use a boneless leg of lamb or thick leg chops. Recipe unsuitable to freeze.

750g boneless chopped lamb
1 tablespoon dark soya sauce
2 teaspoons oil
30g butter
1 medium onion, chopped
1 clove garlic, crushed
1 medium carrot, sliced
1 large potato, chopped
310g can Tomato Supreme
2 sticks celery, sliced
2 tablespoons chopped fresh parsley
2 tablespoons cornflour
¼ cup water

Combine lamb, soya sauce and oil in a bowl. Combine butter, onion and garlic in a large shallow dish, cover, cook on HIGH for 3 minutes. Add lamb, cover, cook on MEDIUM HIGH for 5 minutes. Stir in carrot, potato, Tomato Supreme, celery and parsley, cover, cook on MEDIUM for about 15 minutes or until lamb is just tender, stir occasionally. Stir in blended cornflour and water, cook on HIGH for 3 minutes or until mixture boils and thickens.

Serves 4.

Bowls: John Dermer, Pottery, Yackandandah; tiles: Pazotti

LEFT: Top: Old-Fashioned Lamb and Vegetable Casserole; bottom: Kidneys in Madeira Sauce. BELOW: Lemon and Apricot Racks of Lamb.

KIDNEYS IN MADEIRA SAUCE

Recipe unsuitable to freeze.

12 lambs' kidneys
30g butter
1 medium onion, chopped
2 teaspoons chopped fresh thyme
3 bacon rashers, chopped
1 tablespoon tomato paste
2 teaspoons Worcestershire sauce
2 tablespoons madeira or dry sherry
100g baby mushrooms, sliced
2 teaspoons plain flour
2 tablespoons water

Soak kidneys in cold water for 30 minutes, remove membranes, halve kidneys lengthways and remove centres.

Combine butter in a large shallow dish with the onion, thyme and bacon, cover, cook on HIGH for 3 minutes. Add kidneys to onion mixture, cover, cook on HIGH for 4 minutes, stir occasionally.

Stir in combined tomato paste, sauce and madeira, cover, cook on HIGH for 5 minutes, stir occasionally. Add mushrooms to dish, cover, cook on HIGH for 1 minute. Blend flour and water, stir into kidney mixture, cook on HIGH for about 3 minutes or until the mixture boils and thickens; stir occasionally during cooking.

Serves 4.

China: Limoges; background: Wilson Fabrics

TAMARIND LAMB WITH CORIANDER

Recipe unsuitable to freeze.

1kg lamb chump chops
2 medium potatoes, chopped
1 clove garlic, crushed
2 teaspoons ground cumin
¼ cup tamarind sauce
1 tablespoon dark soya sauce
¾ cup hot water
1 small beef stock cube, crumbled
2 teaspoons sugar
3 green shallots, chopped
1 medium red pepper, chopped
1 tablespoon cornflour
2 tablespoons water, extra
2 teaspoons chopped fresh coriander

Trim excess fat and bones from chops, cut meat in cubes. Combine cubes with potatoes, garlic and cumin in a large shallow dish, cover, cook on HIGH for 6 minutes, stir halfway through cooking time; drain away excess liquid.

Stir in combined sauces, hot water, stock cube, sugar, shallots and pepper, cover, cook on HIGH for 2 minutes. Stir in blended cornflour and extra water, cook on HIGH for about 3 minutes or until mixture boils and thickens. Serve lamb sprinkled with coriander.

Serves 4.

YOGHURT LAMB WITH CASHEWS

Recipe unsuitable to freeze.

1kg lamb leg chops
1 teaspoon paprika
3 teaspoons ground cumin
2 teaspoons ground cardamom
1 clove garlic, crushed
1 small fresh red chilli, chopped
pinch saffron powder
1 cup unroasted unsalted cashew nuts
1 cup plain yoghurt
1 medium onion, chopped
2 medium carrots, chopped
½ cup frozen peas

Trim excess fat and bones from chops, cut meat into cubes. Blend or process paprika, cumin, cardamom, garlic, chilli, saffron, nuts and yoghurt until smooth. Heat a browning dish, place lamb and onion on browning dish, stir until lamb is browned. Stir yoghurt mixture and carrots into lamb mixture, cook on HIGH for 5 minutes, stir occasionally. Stir in peas, cook on HIGH for about 3 minutes or until tender.

Serves 4.

China: Limoges; tray and bowl: Made in Japan

Rectangular dish: Mikasa; background: Wilson Fabrics

SPAGHETTI LAMB PIE

Mince or process boneless chopped lamb. Recipe unsuitable to freeze.

125g spaghetti
1 litre (4 cups) hot water
2 tablespoons grated parmesan cheese
2 eggs
30g butter
1 medium onion, finely chopped
1 small carrot, finely chopped
1 stick celery, finely chopped
½ cup frozen green peas
500g minced lamb
2 tablespoons tomato sauce
2 teaspoons chilli sauce
¼ cup instant potato flakes
pinch dried mixed herbs
1 tablespoon grated parmesan cheese, extra

Break spaghetti in half, place in a large shallow dish, add the water, cook on HIGH for 10 minutes; stir occasionally. Stand a few minutes before draining.

Combine spaghetti with parmesan cheese and one of the eggs. Press spaghetti evenly over base and side of greased 20cm pie plate. Cover pie plate, cook on HIGH for about 2 minutes or until spaghetti mixture is set. Combine butter, onion, carrot, celery and peas in large shallow dish, cover, cook on HIGH for 3 minutes. Stir in lamb, sauces, potato flakes, herbs and remaining egg; mix well.

Spoon into prepared pie plate, sprinkle with extra parmesan cheese, cook on HIGH for about 10 minutes or until cooked through, stand 5 minutes before cutting.

CURRIED LAMB CASSEROLE

Cooked casserole can be frozen for up to 2 months.

30g butter
1 medium onion, finely chopped
1 tablespoon curry powder
2 tablespoons plain flour
2 teaspoons brown sugar
6 large lamb shanks
1 medium potato, chopped
1 large carrot, thinly sliced
1 stick celery, sliced
1 medium apple, grated
1½ cups hot water
1 small beef stock cube, crumbled
1 tablespoon chopped fresh mint
1 tablespoon lemon juice

Combine butter and onion in a large deep dish, cover, cook on HIGH for 3 minutes. Stir in curry powder, flour and sugar, cook on HIGH for 1 minute.

Add shanks, vegetables and apple to dish, cook on HIGH for 4 minutes; stir occasionally. Stir in water, stock cube and mint, cover, cook on MEDIUM for about 35 minutes or until shanks are tender; stir occasionally. Stir in lemon juice. Cover and stand 5 minutes before serving.

Serves 4.

ABOVE: Left: Curried Lamb Casserole; right: Spaghetti Lamb Pie. LEFT: Top: Tamarind Lamb with Coriander; bottom: Yoghurt Lamb with Cashews.

APRICOT PECAN LOIN OF LAMB

Ask the butcher to remove the bone from the loin for you, and to leave a long flap for seasoning and rolling. Recipe can be frozen for up to 2 months.

4 slices bread
15g butter
1 teaspoon French mustard
½ cup stale breadcrumbs
½ cup chopped dried apricots
¼ cup chopped pecans or walnuts
2 teaspoons chopped fresh thyme
1 egg, lightly beaten
1 loin of lamb (4 chops)
1 tablespoon red currant jelly
1 small chicken stock cube, crumbled
½ cup hot water
¼ cup dry red wine
2 teaspoons chopped fresh thyme, extra
2 teaspoons cornflour
1 tablespoon water, extra

Using round cutter (9cm diameter) cut out 4 rounds from bread slices. Combine butter and mustard, spread over both sides of bread, place in a single layer in a large shallow dish, cook on HIGH for 2 minutes, turning once.

Combine breadcrumbs, apricots, pecans, thyme and egg in a bowl; mix well. Place this seasoning along flap of loin, roll up and tie securely with string in 4 separate sections. Cut loin into 4 equal pieces, place in a single layer in a large shallow dish, cover, cook on HIGH for about 15 minutes or until the lamb is cooked as desired; turn occasionally. Remove lamb from dish, cover with foil to keep warm.

Add jelly, stock cube, hot water, wine and extra thyme to dish, cover, cook on HIGH for 2 minutes. Blend cornflour with extra water, stir into dish, cover, cook on HIGH for about 3 minutes or until mixture boils and thickens; stir occasionally. Place bread slices on serving plates, place lamb on bread and top with sauce.

Serves 4.

LAMB WITH PLUM SAUCE

Plum purée is an imported product available from delicatessens. Noisettes are loin chops with the bone removed and the tail curled around the meat. Recipe unsuitable to freeze.

1 tablespoon tomato paste
2 tablespoons honey
2 teaspoons hoisin sauce
1 tablespoon plum purée
4 lamb noisettes
2 teaspoons cornflour
1 tablespoon water
2 teaspoons chopped fresh parsley

Combine tomato paste, honey, hoisin sauce and plum purée in small bowl, cook on HIGH for 30 seconds. Brush noisettes with plum mixture, stand 2 hours or refrigerate overnight.

Place noisettes in a single layer in a shallow dish, cook on HIGH for 9 minutes, turn noisettes once during cooking. Remove noisettes from dish and place on serving plates.

Add blended cornflour and water to liquid in dish, cook on HIGH for about 2 minutes or until mixture boils and thickens, stir occasionally. Serve sauce over noisettes, sprinkle with parsley just before serving.

Serves 4.

Plates and background: Made in Japan

BELOW: Rosemary and Garlic Lamb. LEFT: Top: Apricot Pecan Loin of Lamb; bottom: Lamb with Plum Sauce.

ROSEMARY AND GARLIC LAMB

Ask the butcher to remove the bone from the leg of lamb for you. Recipe unsuitable to freeze.

1½kg leg of lamb, boned
1 tablespoon honey
1 tablespoon tomato paste
1 tablespoon dark soya sauce
6 medium potatoes
3 medium carrots, chopped
2 sprigs fresh rosemary
4 cloves garlic
1 teaspoon dark soya sauce, extra
3 teaspoons mint jelly
1 tablespoon cornflour
2 tablespoons water

Trim excess fat from lamb. Combine honey, tomato paste and sauce in a bowl. Spread lamb out flat, brush with honey mixture.

Cut about 3cm off oven bag from the open end; this cut-off piece is used to tie up the oven bag. Place lamb in oven bag with potatoes, carrots, rosemary and garlic, tie up oven bag.

Place bag in a large shallow dish, cook on MEDIUM HIGH for about 20 minutes. Remove bag carefully from oven. Transfer lamb and vegetables to serving plate; discard rosemary and garlic, cover plate with foil. Reserve liquid in bag.

Combine reserved liquid, extra sauce and mint jelly in a bowl, cover, cook on HIGH for 2 minutes. Stir in blended cornflour and water, cook on HIGH for about 3 minutes or until mixture boils and thickens; stir occasionally. Serve the sauce with lamb and vegetables.

Serves 6.

Platter: Limoges; tiles: Pazotti

CHICKEN

One of the delicate meats, chicken cooks so quickly in the microwave oven that it is better to undercook, then test and continue cooking for short periods until it is done to your taste. Most of these recipes are meant to be cooked and served immediately.

China: Incorporated Agencies

Dish: Inini

PINEAPPLE CITRUS CHICKEN

Recipe unsuitable to freeze.

1½kg chicken pieces
2 tablespoons light soya sauce
1 tablespoon oil
1 clove garlic, crushed
2 teaspoons grated fresh ginger
450g can pineapple pieces
1 tablespoon lemon juice
1 tablespoon cornflour
2 tablespoons water

FAR LEFT: Top: Pineapple Citrus Chicken; bottom: Sweet Chicken and Corn Casserole. LEFT: Sesame Mustard Chicken.

3 spring onions, finely sliced
310g can mandarin oranges, drained
½ cup (50g) flaked almonds, toasted

Place chicken skin-side down in a large shallow dish, brush with combined soya sauce, oil, garlic and ginger. Cover with greaseproof paper, cook on HIGH for 10 minutes.

Combine syrup from drained pineapple with lemon juice; turn chicken over, pour liquid over chicken. Cover with paper, cook on HIGH for about 8 minutes or until just tender. Remove chicken pieces, drain away fat.

Stir in blended cornflour and water and onions, cook on HIGH for about 3 minutes or until mixture boils and thickens, stir occasionally. Stir in pineapple pieces, mandarin oranges and chicken. Cook on HIGH for about 3 minutes or until heated through. Serve sprinkled with almonds.

Serves 4.

SESAME MUSTARD CHICKEN

Recipe unsuitable to freeze.

½ cup sour cream
2 tablespoons seeded mustard
1 teaspoon grated orange rind
4 chicken breast fillets
¾ cup sesame seeds, toasted

Combine sour cream, mustard and orange rind in a bowl, add chicken, stir until chicken is well coated. Roll chicken in sesame seeds, place in a large shallow dish in a single layer, cover, cook on HIGH for about 7 minutes or until chicken is tender.

Serves 4.

SWEET CHICKEN AND CORN CASSEROLE

Recipe unsuitable to freeze.

1 large barbecued chicken
1 medium onion, chopped
2 bacon rashers, chopped
60g butter
¼ cup plain flour
2½ cups milk
¼ cup fruit chutney
¼ cup orange juice
¼ cup dry white wine
1 tablespoon honey
310g can corn kernels, drained
250g baby mushrooms

Remove chicken meat from bones, break meat into bite-sized pieces. Cook onion and bacon in bowl on HIGH for 4 minutes. Place butter in shallow dish on HIGH for 1 minute, stir in flour, milk, chutney, juice, wine and honey. Cook on HIGH for about 5 minutes or until mixture boils and thickens, stir occasionally. Stir in chicken, corn and mushrooms, cover, cook on HIGH for about 3 minutes or until heated through.

Serves 4.

Platter: Inini

ABOVE: From left: Prosciutto Chicken with Prune Sauce; Hazelnut Parmesan Chicken. ABOVE LEFT: Drumsticks with Spicy Plum Glaze.

Dishes: Hale Imports

HAZELNUT PARMESAN CHICKEN

Recipe unsuitable to freeze.

4 chicken breast fillets
30g butter, melted
1 cup (130g) roasted hazelnuts, coarsely ground
¾ cup coarsely grated fresh parmesan cheese
2 tablespoons lemon juice

Brush chicken with butter, then toss in combined hazelnuts and cheese. Place chicken in single layer in a shallow dish, cover with absorbent paper, cook on HIGH for about 7 minutes or until chicken is tender, turn chicken during cooking. Sprinkle lemon juice evenly over chicken just before serving.

Serves 4.

PROSCIUTTO CHICKEN WITH PRUNE SAUCE

Chicken and sauce can be prepared separately up to a day ahead. Recipe unsuitable to freeze.

4 chicken breast fillets
4 slices prosciutto
¼ cup chopped seedless prunes (dried plums)
1 tablespoon lemon juice
1 cup water
1 small chicken stock cube, crumbled
2 teaspoons sugar
1 tablespoon cream

Wrap chicken in prosciutto, tuck ends of prosciutto under chicken. Place chicken in single layer in a shallow dish.

Combine prunes, lemon juice, water, stock cube and sugar in a bowl, cover, cook on HIGH for 3 minutes. Blend or process prune mixture until smooth, stir in cream.

Pour prune mixture over chicken, cover, cook on MEDIUM for about 4 minutes or until chicken is tender, turn during cooking.

Serves 4.

DRUMSTICKS WITH SPICY PLUM GLAZE

Recipe unsuitable to freeze.

½ cup plum sauce
1 tablespoon light soya sauce
1 tablespoon hoisin sauce
½ teaspoon tabasco sauce
2 tablespoons dry sherry
1 teaspoon oil
2 teaspoons sugar
10 chicken drumsticks
1 tablespoon oil, extra
3 teaspoons cornflour
¼ cup water

Combine sauces, sherry, oil and sugar in a large bowl with chicken, cover, marinate in refrigerator several hours or overnight.

Drain chicken, reserve marinade. Heat extra oil in a large shallow dish on HIGH for 1 minute, add chicken, cook on HIGH for about 12 minutes or until chicken is tender; turn chicken several times during cooking. Combine reserved marinade with blended cornflour and water, pour over chicken, cook on HIGH for about 3 minutes or until mixture boils and thickens.

Serves 4.

CHICKEN

DEVILLED CHICKEN DRUMETTES

Drumettes are the meaty end of drumsticks. Recipe unsuitable to freeze.

15g butter
¼ cup tomato sauce
1 tablespoon light soya sauce
2 teaspoons Worcestershire sauce
2 tablespoons fruit chutney
2 tablespoons brown sugar
1 teaspoon curry powder
750g chicken drumettes

Melt butter in a bowl on HIGH for 15 seconds, stir in sauces, chutney, sugar and curry powder. Add chicken, cover, marinate in refrigerator several hours or overnight. Place chicken in a single layer in a shallow dish with marinade, cook on HIGH for about 12 minutes or until tender, stir occasionally. Serve hot or cold.

Serves 4.

Dish: Accoutrement

Platter: Decor Gifts

CAMEMBERT PASTRAMI CHICKEN

Ham can be substituted for pastrami. Recipe unsuitable to freeze.

4 chicken breast fillets
125g camembert cheese, quartered
50g pastrami, chopped

TOMATO BASIL SAUCE

30g butter
1 medium onion, chopped
1 clove garlic, crushed
425g can tomatoes
1 tablespoon tomato paste
¼ cup water
¼ cup dry white wine
1 small chicken stock cube, crumbled
1 teaspoon Worcestershire sauce
1 tablespoon chopped fresh basil

Cut a slit in the thickest part of the side of each fillet to form a pocket. Fill each pocket with cheese and pastrami; secure opening with toothpicks. Place fillets in a single layer in a shallow dish, cover, cook on HIGH for about 5 minutes or until chicken is tender; turn chicken during cooking time. Serve chicken with sauce.

Tomato Basil Sauce: Combine butter, onion and garlic in a large bowl, cover, cook on HIGH for 3 minutes. Add undrained crushed tomatoes, tomato paste, water, wine, stock cube and sauce, cover, cook on HIGH for 12 minutes, stir in basil before serving.

Serves 4.

FAR LEFT: Devilled Chicken Drumettes. LEFT: Camembert Pastrami Chicken. BELOW: Chicken with Peppers.

CHICKEN WITH PEPPERS

Recipe unsuitable to freeze.

30g butter
1 tablespoon oil
1 medium onion, sliced
1 clove garlic, crushed
1 medium red pepper, sliced
1 medium green pepper, sliced
4 chicken breast fillets
½ cup dry white wine
2 teaspoons chopped fresh oregano
1 tablespoon cornflour
¼ cup water

Combine butter, oil, onion and garlic in a large shallow dish, cover, cook on HIGH for 3 minutes. Stir in peppers, cover, cook on HIGH for 3 minutes. Place chicken on top of peppers, add wine and oregano, cover, cook on HIGH for about 7 minutes or until chicken is tender; turn during cooking.

Blend cornflour with water, stir into chicken mixture, cover, cook on HIGH for about 2 minutes or until mixture boils and thickens, stir occasionally.

Serves 4.

Dish: Inini

China: The Bay Tree

DRUMSTICKS WITH HERBED CRUMB CRUST

Recipe unsuitable to freeze.

2 teaspoons dry mustard
1 cup plain flour
2 eggs
2 tablespoons milk
¾ cup packaged breadcrumbs
1 tablespoon chopped fresh chives
1 tablespoon chopped fresh thyme
1 tablespoon chopped fresh parsley
8 chicken drumsticks

Combine mustard and flour in a bowl. Beat eggs and milk together in a bowl. Mix breadcrumbs and herbs in a bowl.

Toss chicken in flour mixture, dip into egg mixture, toss in breadcrumb mixture. Place chicken in a single layer in a large shallow dish, cook on HIGH for about 12 minutes or until tender, turn chicken once during cooking.

Serves 4.

CREAMY APPLE AND BACON DRUMSTICKS

Recipe unsuitable to freeze.

8 chicken drumsticks
30g butter
1 onion, sliced
2 bacon rashers, sliced
185g can apple sauce
2 tablespoons apple juice
¾ cup cream
1 tablespoon cornflour
1 tablespoon water
1 tablespoon chopped fresh parsley

Remove skin from drumsticks. Combine butter, onion and bacon in a large shallow dish, cover, cook on HIGH for 3 minutes. Add chicken, apple sauce, juice and cream, cover, cook on HIGH for about 9 minutes or until chicken is tender, turn chicken several times during cooking. Remove chicken from dish, cover to keep hot.

Blend cornflour with water, add to dish, cook on HIGH for about 2 minutes or until mixture boils and thickens, stir occasionally. Add chicken, serve sprinkled with parsley.

Serves 4.

CHICKEN AND MUSHROOMS IN RED WINE

Recipe unsuitable to freeze.

No. 15 chicken
60g butter
4 bacon rashers, chopped
2 medium onions, quartered
2 cloves garlic, crushed
1 cup dry red wine
1 cup water
1 small chicken stock cube, crumbled
1 tablespoon brandy
¼ cup tomato purée
250g baby mushrooms
1 tablespoon plain flour
2 tablespoons water, extra

Cut chicken into serving-sized pieces, remove any fat and skin.

Melt butter in a large shallow dish on HIGH for 1 minute. Add chicken in a single layer, cook on HIGH for 4 minutes, turn chicken during cooking, remove from dish, drain away fat. Add bacon, onions and garlic to dish, cover, cook on HIGH for 4 minutes, stir occasionally. Stir in wine, water, stock cube, brandy, tomato purée and chicken, cook on HIGH for about 15

Bowls: Inini

minutes, stir occasionally. Add mushrooms, cook on HIGH for about 10 minutes or until chicken is tender.

Remove chicken, cover to keep hot. Stir blended flour and extra water into dish, cover, cook on HIGH for about 3 minutes or until mixture boils and thickens, stir occasionally, serve over chicken.

Serves 4.

CHICKEN, TOMATO AND LEEK CASSEROLE

Recipe unsuitable to freeze.

30g butter
1 medium leek, sliced
1 clove garlic, crushed
310g can Tomato Supreme
1 medium zucchini, sliced
¼ cup dry white wine
6 chicken thigh fillets, chopped
185g mushrooms, sliced
2 tablespoons chopped fresh parsley

Combine butter, leek and garlic in a large bowl, cover, cook on HIGH for 3 minutes. Add Tomato Supreme, zucchini and wine, cover, cook on HIGH for 5 minutes. Stir in chicken, mushrooms and parsley, cover, cook on HIGH for about 7 minutes or until chicken is tender, stir occasionally.

Serves 4.

ABOVE: Top: Chicken and Mushrooms in Red Wine; bottom: Chicken, Tomato and Leek Casserole. ABOVE LEFT: From left: Drumsticks with Herbed Crumb Crust; Creamy Apple and Bacon Drumsticks.

CHICKEN WITH HAZELNUT CREAM SAUCE

Recipe unsuitable to freeze.

4 chicken breast fillets
15g butter
1 tablespoon dry white wine
½ cup cream
½ small chicken stock cube, crumbled
1 teaspoon cornflour
1 teaspoon water
2 tablespoons chopped roasted hazelnuts
1 tablespoon chopped fresh parsley

Cut chicken into bite-sized pieces. Melt butter in a large shallow dish on HIGH for 15 seconds, add chicken, cover, cook on HIGH for 4 minutes; stir occasionally.

Combine wine, cream and stock cube in a bowl, cook on HIGH for 3 minutes. Add blended cornflour and water, cook on HIGH for about 2 minutes or until sauce boils and thickens. Add chicken, hazelnuts and parsley. Cook on HIGH for about 1 minute or until heated through.

Serves 4.

CHICKEN WITH SWEET ORANGE GLAZE

Recipe unsuitable to freeze.

15g butter
1 teaspoon grated orange rind
¼ cup orange juice
¼ cup red currant jelly
1 small chicken stock cube, crumbled
2 tablespoons port
4 chicken half breasts on the bone
3 teaspoons cornflour
2 tablespoons water

Combine butter, orange rind and juice, jelly, stock cube and port in a large bowl, cook on HIGH for 1 minute. Add chicken, mix well, cover, marinate in refrigerator several hours.

Remove chicken from marinade, place into a shallow dish in a single layer; reserve marinade. Cook chicken on HIGH for about 10 minutes or until chicken is tender; turn during cooking. Combine reserved marinade with blended cornflour and water in a bowl, cook on HIGH for about 3 minutes or until mixture boils and thickens, serve over chicken.

Serves 4.

RIGHT: Top: Chicken Breasts with Red Currant Glaze; bottom: Pepper and Peanut Chicken. BELOW: From left: Chicken with Sweet Orange Glaze; Chicken with Hazelnut Cream Sauce.

Table: Alcan Aluminium

China: Incorporated Agencies; table: Alcan Aluminium

CHICKEN BREASTS WITH RED CURRANT GLAZE

Sauce can be prepared up to 2 days ahead. Recipe unsuitable to freeze.

15g butter
1 tablespoon dry sherry
4 chicken breast fillets
RED CURRANT GLAZE
2 tablespoons red currant jelly
½ cup water
½ small chicken stock cube, crumbled
1 teaspoon grated lemon rind
2 tablespoons lemon juice
100g fresh or frozen red currants
2 teaspoons cornflour
2 teaspoons water, extra

Melt butter in a shallow dish on HIGH for 15 seconds, add sherry and chicken in a single layer, cover, cook on HIGH for 6 minutes, turn chicken during cooking. Cover to keep hot.

Red Currant Glaze: Combine jelly, water, stock cube, rind and juice and red currants in a bowl, cover, cook on HIGH for 1 minute. Stir in blended cornflour and extra water, cook on HIGH for about 2 minutes or until mixture boils and thickens; serve glaze over chicken.

Serves 4.

PEPPER AND PEANUT CHICKEN

Recipe unsuitable to freeze.

1 teaspoon sesame oil
15g butter
1 clove garlic, crushed
1 medium onion, sliced
500g chicken thigh fillets, sliced
2 tablespoons crunchy peanut butter
½ teaspoon ground cardamom
1 teaspoon ground cumin
2 tablespoons light soya sauce
3 teaspoons honey
1 tablespoon lime juice
1 medium red pepper, chopped
1 medium green pepper, chopped
250g bean sprouts

Combine oil, butter, garlic and onion in a large shallow dish, cook on HIGH for 3 minutes. Stir in chicken, cover, cook on HIGH for 3 minutes. Stir in combined peanut butter, cardamom, cumin, soya sauce, honey and lime juice, cover, cook on HIGH for 3 minutes; stir once during cooking. Stir in peppers, cook on HIGH for 1 minute. Serve with bean sprouts.

Serves 4.

PEPPERED CHICKEN WITH CREAMY SAUCE

Recipe unsuitable to freeze.

30g butter
1 clove garlic, crushed
4 chicken breast fillets
2 tablespoons cracked black peppercorns
30g butter, extra
2 tablespoons plain flour
1 small chicken stock cube, crumbled
¾ cup cream
¼ cup dry white wine
1 tablespoon marsala

Combine butter and garlic in a small bowl, cook on HIGH for about 30 seconds or until butter is melted. Brush chicken with butter mixture, then toss in peppercorns.

Place chicken in a single layer in a shallow dish. Cook on HIGH for 3 minutes, turn chicken during cooking time.

Melt extra butter in a small bowl on HIGH for about 30 seconds, stir in flour, stock cube, cream, wine and marsala. Pour over chicken, cook on HIGH for about 6 minutes or until sauce boils and thickens and chicken is tender; turn chicken and stir sauce several times during the cooking time.

Serves 4.

ABOVE: Peppered Chicken with Creamy Sauce. RIGHT: Chicken Casserole with Herbed Dumplings. BELOW: Corn 'n' Raisin Chicken.

CORN 'N' RAISIN CHICKEN

Recipe unsuitable to freeze.

60g butter
1 tablespoon light soya sauce
No. 15 chicken
2 bacon rashers, chopped
2 cups stale breadcrumbs
2 tablespoons pine nuts
2 tablespoons chopped fresh parsley
130g can creamed corn
1 tablespoon chopped raisins
1 egg, lightly beaten

Melt butter in bowl on HIGH for 1 minute, add soya sauce. Brush skin of chicken all over with soya sauce mixture. Cook bacon in a bowl on HIGH for 3 minutes, stir in breadcrumbs, pine nuts, parsley, corn, raisins and egg.

Fill chicken cavity with seasoning mixture, secure opening with skewer. Tuck wings under chicken body. Place chicken on a flat dish, cook on HIGH for 15 minutes, basting occasionally. Turn chicken over, cook on HIGH for 15 minutes, cover, stand 10 minutes before serving.

Serves 4.

Casserole dish: Mosmania

CHICKEN CASSEROLE WITH HERBED DUMPLINGS

We used fresh thyme to flavour this dish, but any of your favourite herbs can be substituted. Casserole can be prepared up to a day ahead or can be frozen for up to 2 months.

60g butter
1 medium red pepper, chopped
1 medium green pepper, chopped
1 medium onion, sliced
1 clove garlic, crushed
2 teaspoons chopped fresh thyme
4 chicken maryland pieces
1 small chicken stock cube, crumbled
1 cup water
425g can tomatoes
2 tablespoons tomato paste
200g baby mushrooms, sliced
2 tablespoons cornflour
¼ cup water, extra

HERBED DUMPLINGS

½ cup self-raising flour
30g butter
1 tablespoon chopped fresh thyme
2 tablespoons water, approximately

Combine butter, peppers, onion, garlic and thyme in a large shallow dish, cover, cook on HIGH for 3 minutes. Add chicken to dish, cover, cook on HIGH for 5 minutes. Stir in stock cube, water, undrained crushed tomatoes, tomato paste and mushrooms, cover, cook on HIGH for 15 minutes.

Add dumplings, cover, cook on HIGH for 7 minutes or until chicken is tender. Remove dumplings.

Stir blended cornflour and extra water into chicken mixture, cover, cook on HIGH for about 3 minutes or until mixture boils and thickens, stir occasionally. Return dumplings to chicken mixture, reheat if necessary.

Herbed Dumplings: Sift flour into a bowl, rub in butter, add thyme, then enough water to flour mixture to mix to a soft dough. Shape mixture into 4 dumplings using floured hands.

Serves 4.

COUNTRY CHICKEN TERRINE

Terrine can be made a day ahead of serving. Recipe unsuitable to freeze.

½ bunch English spinach (20 leaves)
100g lambs' kidneys, finely chopped
250g chicken livers, finely chopped
250g lean pork, finely chopped
1 tablespoon port
1 teaspoon grated orange rind
1 tablespoon orange juice
30g butter
1 small onion, finely chopped
3 bacon rashers, finely chopped
¼ teaspoon dried basil leaves
¼ teaspoon dried thyme leaves
1 tablespoon canned green peppercorns, drained
1 cup stale white breadcrumbs
1 egg, lightly beaten

Place rinsed spinach leaves in a large bowl, cover, cook on HIGH for about 1 minute or until leaves are just wilted. Rinse spinach under cold water, drain well. Line base and side of a 3 cup capacity dish with spinach, reserve about 4 leaves to cover the top.

Combine kidneys, livers, pork, port, orange rind and juice in a bowl, mix well. Combine butter and onion in a large bowl, cover, cook on HIGH for 3 minutes, stir in meat mixture and bacon, cook on HIGH for 10 minutes, stir during cooking.

Stand 10 minutes before stirring in remaining ingredients. Press mixture into prepared dish, cover with reserved spinach. Cover dish, cook on MEDIUM for 6 minutes. Cool to room temperature, cover with plastic wrap, weight with a plate topped with unopened cans of food. Refrigerate overnight.

BACON, RICOTTA AND CHICKEN ROLLS

Recipe unsuitable to freeze.

3 bacon rashers, finely chopped
1 cup (200g) ricotta cheese
2 tablespoons currants
2 tablespoons chopped fresh chives
4 chicken breast fillets
¼ cup lemon juice
½ cup orange juice
3 teaspoons sugar
30g butter, chopped
1½ teaspoons cornflour
1 tablespoon water

Place bacon in a bowl, cook on HIGH for 2 minutes, drain, cook on HIGH further 1 minute, drain.

Combine bacon, cheese, currants and chives in a large bowl. Pound chicken with meat mallet until thin. Divide ricotta mixture evenly over chicken, fold in sides of each fillet, roll fillets up neatly.

Place chicken, seam side down, in a single layer in a shallow dish. Add combined juices and sugar, cover, cook on MEDIUM for about 5 minutes or until chicken is tender. Remove chicken from dish, cover to keep hot.

Stir butter into hot orange juice mixture, stir in blended cornflour and water, cover, cook on HIGH for about 3 minutes or until sauce boils and thickens. Serve over chicken.

Serves 4.

RIGHT: Country Chicken Terrine.
BELOW: Bacon, Ricotta and Chicken Rolls.

Platter: Incorporated Agencies; table: Alcan Aluminium

DESSERTS

Desserts both hot and cold abound in this section, also a super selection of sauces to serve over fruit or ice-cream. Some great cakes which will please the most discerning cake cooks are also included — these are always at their best if eaten on the day they are made.

STRAWBERRY MALLOW CREAMS

This recipe can be made up to one day ahead; it is not suitable to freeze.

2 teaspoons gelatine
1 tablespoon water
100g packet pink marshmallows
2 tablespoons lemon juice
250g punnet strawberries
200g carton strawberry yoghurt
½ cup thickened cream

Sprinkle gelatine over the water in a large bowl, add marshmallows and lemon juice, cook on HIGH for 1 minute, remove from oven, stir until marshmallows are melted.

Blend or process strawberries, stir into marshmallow mixture with yoghurt and cream. Pour mixture into 4 dishes (three-quarter cup capacity). Refrigerate several hours or until set.

Serves 4.

Glassware: Dansab; tiles: Northbridge Ceramic & Marble Centre

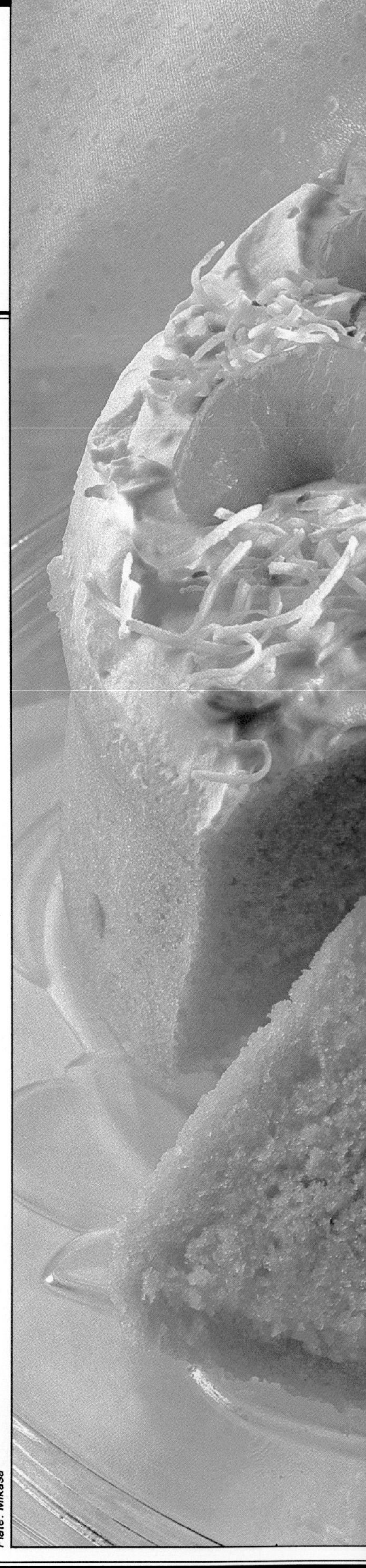

Plate: Mikasa

PINEAPPLE SYRUP CAKE

Recipe unsuitable to freeze.

125g butter
2 teaspoons grated lemon rind
¾ cup castor sugar
2 eggs
1 cup self-raising flour
⅓ cup plain flour
⅓ cup pineapple juice
¼ cup milk
PINEAPPLE SYRUP
⅔ cup pineapple juice
1 tablespoon lemon juice
½ cup sugar

Grease a 21cm ring dish. Cream butter, rind and sugar in a small bowl with electric mixer until light and fluffy, beat in eggs one at a time, beat until combined. Stir in half the sifted flours with the pineapple juice, then stir in remaining flours and milk. Spread mixture into prepared dish, cook on MEDIUM HIGH for about 11 minutes or until cake feels firm to the touch. Stand cake in dish while making the syrup.

Pour hot syrup over hot cake, stand 1 minute before turning onto serving plate. Serve warm or cold with cream.

Pineapple Syrup: Combine all ingredients in small bowl, cook on HIGH for about 3 minutes or until sugar is dissolved, stir occasionally.

LEFT: Pineapple Syrup Cake. FAR LEFT: Strawberry Mallow Creams.

SPICY PUMPKIN PIE

You will need to cook 350g pumpkin for this recipe. Mash until smooth; do not add any milk or butter. Recipe unsuitable to freeze.

CRUMB CRUST
90g butter
1½ cups (185g) plain sweet biscuit crumbs
¼ teaspoon mixed spice
SPICY PUMPKIN FILLING
1 cup mashed pumpkin
½ cup brown sugar, firmly packed
¾ cup sour cream
½ teaspoon mixed spice
½ teaspoon ground ginger
¼ teaspoon ground nutmeg
3 eggs

Crumb Crust: Melt butter in a bowl on HIGH for 1 minute, stir in crumbs and mixed spice. Press crumbs firmly over base and side of a 22cm pie plate, cook on HIGH for 1 minute, cool. Pour filling into crumb crust, cook on MEDIUM HIGH for about 18 minutes or until filling is just set. Stand 10 minutes before cutting. Serve warm or cold.

Spicy Pumpkin Filling: Blend or process all ingredients until smooth.

Top: Spicy Pumpkin Pie; bottom: Mocha Syrup Cake.

Pie plate: Modern Living; plate: Studio-Haus

MOCHA SYRUP CAKE

Tia Maria and Kahlua are coffee-flavoured liqueurs. Recipe unsuitable to freeze.

125g butter
⅔ cup castor sugar
2 eggs
1½ cups self-raising flour
¼ cup cocoa
¾ cup milk
COFFEE SYRUP
¾ cup sugar
¾ cup hot water
1½ tablespoons Tia Maria or Kahlua
1½ tablespoons dry instant coffee
2 tablespoons hot water, extra

Grease a 25cm ring dish. Cream butter and sugar in a small bowl with electric mixer, add eggs one at a time, beat until just combined. Stir in half the sifted dry ingredients with half the milk, then remaining dry ingredients and milk. Pour mixture into prepared dish, cook on HIGH for about 8 minutes or until just firm. Stand 5 minutes before turning onto rack.

Brush hot syrup over hot cake. Dust with icing sugar. Serve with whipped cream and strawberries.

Coffee Syrup: Combine sugar, hot water and liqueur in a small bowl, stir until sugar is dissolved, then cook on HIGH for 3 minutes, stir in combined coffee powder and extra hot water.

COFFEE LIQUEUR CHARLOTTE

Tia Maria and Kahlua are coffee-flavoured liqueurs. Charlotte can be made the day before required. Recipe unsuitable to freeze.

10 savoiardi biscuits
¼ cup warm milk
1 tablespoon Tia Maria or Kahlua
2 tablespoons dry instant coffee
1 cup milk, extra
1 tablespoon gelatine
4 eggs, separated
½ cup castor sugar
2 tablespoons Tia Maria or Kahlua, extra
300ml carton thickened cream

Oil a deep 20cm round cake pan, line base with greaseproof paper, oil paper. Cut savoiardi biscuits crossways in half, brush with combined milk and liqueur. Stand biscuits upright, sugar side out, around side of cake pan, overlapping each biscuit slightly.

Combine coffee and extra milk in a bowl, sprinkle with gelatine, mix well, cook on HIGH for about 1½ minutes or until coffee and gelatine are dissolved.

Beat egg yolks and sugar in small bowl with electric mixer until thick and creamy. Gradually beat in hot milk mixture. Cook on HIGH for 1 minute, cool, refrigerate until mixture has set to the consistency of unbeaten egg white, stir occasionally during chilling. Fold in extra liqueur and cream. Beat egg whites in a small bowl until soft peaks form, fold into mixture. Pour mixture carefully into centre of biscuits in pan, refrigerate until set.

APPLE AND WALNUT CAKE

Recipe unsuitable to freeze.

¼ cup ground roasted hazelnuts
1 cup self-raising flour
¼ teaspoon ground cinnamon
60g butter
⅓ cup brown sugar
⅓ cup chopped walnuts
1 apple, grated
2 eggs, lightly beaten
1 tablespoon golden syrup
¼ cup milk

Grease a 19cm ring dish, sprinkle base and side with hazelnuts. Combine sifted flour and cinnamon in a large bowl, rub in butter. Add sugar, walnuts, apple, eggs and combined golden syrup and milk; mix well.

Pour mixture into prepared dish. Cook on HIGH for about 5 minutes or until just set. Stand 5 minutes before turning onto wire rack to cool. Serve sprinkled with sifted icing sugar.

CHOC-CHIP DESSERT CAKE

Recipe unsuitable to freeze.

125g butter
1 teaspoon vanilla essence
⅔ cup brown sugar
2 eggs
1½ cups self-raising flour
¼ cup cocoa
½ teaspoon bicarbonate of soda
1 cup sour cream
⅓ cup Choc Bits

Grease a 21cm ring dish. Cream butter, essence and sugar in a small bowl with electric mixer, add eggs one at a time, beat until just combined. Stir in half the sifted dry ingredients with half the sour cream, then stir in remaining dry ingredients, sour cream and the Choc Bits.

Pour mixture into prepared dish, cook on HIGH for about 8 minutes or until just set. Stand, covered, for 10 minutes before turning onto serving plate. Serve warm or cold with cream.

BELOW: Left: Choc-Chip Dessert Cake; right: Apple and Walnut Cake. RIGHT: Coffee Liqueur Charlotte.

China: Mikasa; silk flowers: Modern Living

Plate: Incorporated Agencies; table: Alcan Aluminium

ONE-BOWL CHOCOLATE CAKE

Recipe unsuitable to freeze

125g butter
1 cup castor sugar
1 cup water
1½ cups self-raising flour
⅓ cup cocoa
½ teaspoon bicarbonate of soda
2 eggs, lightly beaten

Grease a 23cm ring dish. Combine butter, sugar and water in a large bowl, cook on HIGH for 4 minutes; cool to room temperature. Sift dry ingredients into butter mixture, beat with wooden spoon until smooth; stir in eggs.

Pour mixture into prepared dish, cook on HIGH for about 8 minutes or until cake feels firm. Stand 5 minutes before turning onto wire rack to cool.

CARROT APPLE RING CAKE

Recipe unsuitable to freeze.

1 cup self-raising flour
½ cup full cream milk powder
¾ cup castor sugar
1 cup finely grated carrot
1 medium apple, grated
2 eggs, lightly beaten
½ cup chopped pecans or walnuts
½ cup oil
1 tablespoon chopped pecans or walnuts, extra

CREAM CHEESE FROSTING
30g packaged cream cheese
1½ tablespoons butter
1 teaspoon lemon juice
1 cup icing sugar

Grease a 23cm ring dish. Combine sifted flour, milk powder and sugar in a bowl, add carrot, apple, eggs, nuts and oil, stir until combined.

Pour mixture into prepared dish, cook on HIGH for about 8 minutes or until cake feels firm. Stand 5 minutes, turn onto wire rack to cool. Spread cold cake with frosting, sprinkle with extra nuts.

Cream Cheese Frosting: Beat cream cheese, butter and lemon juice in a small bowl with electric mixer until light and fluffy, gradually beat in sifted icing sugar, beat until smooth.

RIGHT: Top: One-Bowl Chocolate Cake; bottom: Carrot Apple Ring Cake. FAR RIGHT: Chocolate Coffee Gateau.

China: Mikasa; cane tray & silk flowers: Modern Living

Plate: Mikasa

CHOCOLATE COFFEE GATEAU

Kahlua and Tia Maria are coffee-flavoured liqueurs. Recipe unsuitable to freeze.

125g butter
1 teaspoon vanilla essence
¾ cup castor sugar
2 eggs
¾ cup self-raising flour
⅓ cup milk
185g dark chocolate, grated
COFFEE SYRUP
1 tablespoon sugar
2 tablespoons hot water
1 tablespoon Kahlua or Tia Maria
VANILLA CREAM
250g butter
3 cups icing sugar
⅓ cup milk
RICH CHOCOLATE CREAM
1 tablespoon cream
60g dark chocolate, grated

Line base of a 20cm pie plate with absorbent paper. Cream butter, essence and sugar in a small bowl with electric mixer until light and fluffy. Add eggs one at a time, beating well after each addition. Transfer to a large bowl.

Stir in half the sifted flour with half the milk, then stir in remaining flour, half the grated chocolate and remaining milk; stir until combined.

Divide mixture into 3 parts. Spread 1 part evenly into prepared plate, cook on HIGH for 2 minutes, stand 5 minutes before turning onto wire rack. Repeat with remaining mixture; cool layers to room temperature.

To decorate cake, first reserve half the vanilla cream.

Place 1 layer on serving plate, brush with syrup, spread with half the remaining vanilla cream, then half the rich chocolate cream.

Repeat with second layer.

Brush top of cake with syrup, spread cake all over with reserved vanilla cream. Sprinkle remaining grated chocolate over top and side of cake.

Coffee Syrup: Combine sugar and water in a small bowl, cook on HIGH for 30 seconds or until sugar is dissolved, cool to room temperature, add liqueur.

Vanilla Cream: Beat butter in a small bowl with electric mixer until as white as possible; gradually beat in half the sifted icing sugar, then the milk, then remaining icing sugar.

Rich Chocolate Cream: Heat cream in a small bowl on HIGH for 15 seconds, add chocolate, stir until smooth.

ALMOND PEAR PUDDINGS

Recipe unsuitable to freeze.

425g can pear halves, drained
4 teaspoons apricot jam
90g butter
2 tablespoons castor sugar
1 egg
⅔ cup (80g) ground almonds
1 tablespoon self-raising flour
½ teaspoon ground cinnamon
3 teaspoons castor sugar, extra

Place pears into 4 dishes (three-quarter cup capacity), top each pear with a teaspoon of jam. Cream butter and sugar in a small bowl with electric mixer until light and fluffy, add egg, beat until just combined. Stir in almonds and sifted flour. Spread mixture evenly over pears, cook on HIGH for about 5 minutes or until just set. Sprinkle puddings with combined cinnamon and extra sugar. Serve warm with cream or custard.

Serves 4.

APPLE CREAM CRUMBLE

Recipe unsuitable to freeze.

410g can pie apple
¾ cup sour cream
1 tablespoon castor sugar
1 egg
30g butter
1 tablespoon honey
¾ cup toasted muesli
2 tablespoons coconut
2 tablespoons self-raising flour
¼ cup slivered almonds
1 teaspoon grated lemon rind

Spread apple over base of a 20cm pie dish. Combine sour cream, sugar and egg in a bowl, beat with a fork until just combined, pour over apple, cook on MEDIUM for 6 minutes; stand while preparing topping.

Combine butter and honey in a bowl, cook on HIGH for 1 minute, stir in remaining ingredients, cook on HIGH for 2 minutes, stir occasionally. Stand 5 minutes before sprinkling over sour cream mixture, then cook on HIGH for about 2 minutes or until heated through. Serve warm with cream or ice-cream.

Serves 4.

TANGY PLUM WATER ICE

Ice can be prepared 3 days ahead.

12 medium (1kg) blood plums, seeded
¾ cup castor sugar
1 tablespoon grated orange rind
¾ cup orange juice
½ cup dry white wine

Blend or process plums until smooth, strain to remove skin.

Combine all ingredients in a large bowl, cover, cook on HIGH for 3 minutes, stir until sugar is dissolved. Cover, cook on HIGH for 3 minutes, pour into loaf pan, cool to room temperature. Cover pan with foil, freeze several hours or until icy around the edges. Remove from freezer, mix well with a fork, cover, return to freezer until set.

Serves 4.

BELOW: Tangy Plum Water Ice.
RIGHT: Top: Almond Pear Puddings; bottom: Apple Cream Crumble.

China: Villeroy & Boch; fabric: Wilson; tiles: Pazotti

Tiles: Northbridge Ceramic & Marble Centre

Table: Alcan Aluminium

ABOVE: Whisky Cream Mousse.
RIGHT: Orange Raisin Puddings.

WHISKY CREAM MOUSSE

Mousse can be prepared up to 3 days ahead. Recipe unsuitable to freeze.

1 teaspoon gelatine
2 teaspoons dry coffee powder
2 tablespoons water
300ml carton thickened cream
2 tablespoons icing sugar
¼ cup Baileys Original Irish Cream

Combine gelatine, coffee and water in a small bowl, cook on HIGH for about 20 seconds or until gelatine is dissolved, cool, do not allow to set. Whip cream and sifted icing sugar until soft peaks form, fold in gelatine mixture and Baileys; pour into 4 dishes (one-third cup capacity), refrigerate.

Serves 4.

ORANGE RAISIN PUDDINGS

Recipe unsuitable to freeze.

90g butter
1 tablespoon grated orange rind
½ cup brown sugar, firmly packed
2 eggs
¾ cup stale wholemeal breadcrumbs
1 cup (170g) chopped raisins
1 cup self-raising flour
½ cup orange juice

CREAMY ORANGE SAUCE

30g butter
1 tablespoon custard powder
¼ cup castor sugar
½ cup cream
2 teaspoons grated orange rind
½ cup orange juice

Grease 4 dishes (1 cup capacity). Cream butter, rind and sugar in a small bowl with electric mixer until light and fluffy. Add eggs one at a time, beat until combined. Stir in breadcrumbs and raisins. Stir in half the sifted flour and half the juice, then remaining flour and juice.

Spoon into prepared dishes, cook on MEDIUM for about 5 minutes or until just set. Stand 2 minutes before turning onto plates; serve with sauce.

Creamy Orange Sauce: Melt butter in a bowl on HIGH for 30 seconds. Stir in custard powder, sugar, cream, orange rind and juice. Cook on HIGH for about 3 minutes or until mixture boils and thickens; stir occasionally.

Serves 4.

APRICOT PUDDINGS WITH LEMON CREAM SAUCE

We used ordinary teacups for the cooking of these puddings. Recipe unsuitable to freeze.

⅔ cup (100g) chopped dried apricots
1 cup hot water
60g butter
1 cup self-raising flour
¼ teaspoon bicarbonate of soda
½ cup castor sugar
2 tablespoons water, extra
1 egg, lightly beaten
1 teaspoon grated lemon rind
LEMON CREAM SAUCE
3 teaspoons cornflour
½ cup water
⅓ cup sugar
⅔ cup cream
1 teaspoon grated lemon rind
1 tablespoon lemon juice

Grease 4 dishes (three-quarter cup capacity). Combine apricots and water in a bowl, cover, cook on HIGH for 4 minutes; drain.

Melt butter in a bowl on HIGH for 1 minute. Add sifted flour and soda, apricots, sugar, extra water, egg and lemon rind, mix well. Spoon mixture evenly into prepared dishes, cover, cook on MEDIUM for about 6 minutes or until set. Stand puddings, covered, 5 minutes before turning onto serving plates. Serve with sauce.

Lemon Cream Sauce: Combine blended cornflour and water with remaining ingredients in a bowl, cook on HIGH for about 3 minutes or until sauce boils and thickens, stir occasionally.

Serves 4.

MARSHMALLOW CARAMEL SAUCE

Sauce can be made up to 3 days ahead; reheat before serving. Recipe unsuitable to freeze.

125g butter
¾ cup brown sugar, firmly packed
100g packet white marshmallows
2 tablespoons milk

Combine butter, brown sugar, marshmallows and milk in a large bowl, cook on HIGH for about 3 minutes or until marshmallows are melted; stir occasionally. Serve warm over ice-cream.

Makes about 1½ cups.

Tiles: Northbridge Ceramic & Marble Centre

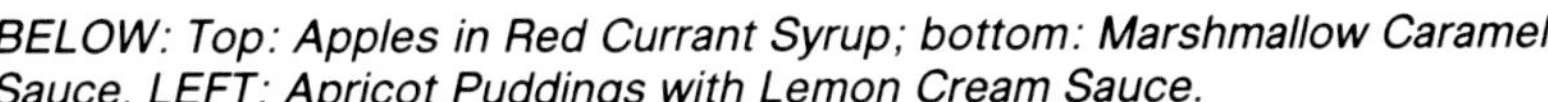

BELOW: Top: Apples in Red Currant Syrup; bottom: Marshmallow Caramel Sauce. LEFT: Apricot Puddings with Lemon Cream Sauce.

APPLES IN RED CURRANT SYRUP

Dessert can be made up to 2 days ahead. Recipe unsuitable to freeze.

2 Granny Smith apples, quartered
125g fresh or frozen red currants
60g fresh or frozen black currants
⅓ cup orange juice
2 tablespoons castor sugar

Combine apples in a large bowl with currants and orange juice, cover, cook on HIGH for 3 minutes. Stir in sugar, cover, cook on HIGH for about 3 minutes or until apples are tender. Cool, cover, refrigerate for about 2 hours or overnight before serving.

Serves 4.

Glasses: Orrefors; china: Crabtree & Evelyn; tiles: Northbridge Ceramic & Marble Centre

Dish: Incorporated Agencies

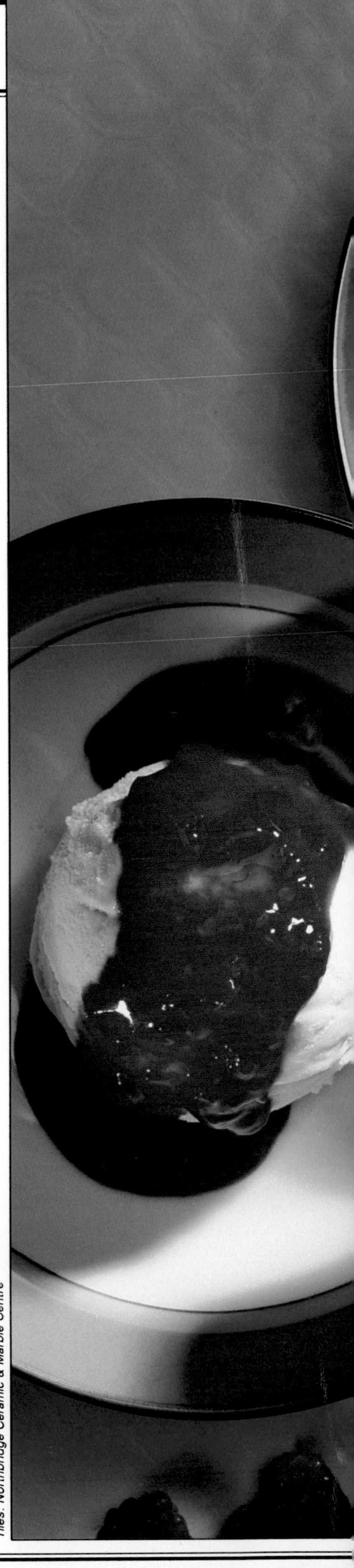

Tiles: Northbridge Ceramic & Marble Centre

CREAMY ORANGE SAUCE WITH FRUIT

Grand Marnier is a citrus-flavoured liqueur. Recipe unsuitable to freeze.

3 egg yolks
¼ cup castor sugar
½ teaspoon grated orange rind
2 teaspoons orange juice
2 teaspoons Grand Marnier

Combine egg yolks, sugar and rind in a small bowl of electric mixer, beat on medium speed until thick and creamy. Add orange juice and liqueur. Transfer mixture to a large bowl, cook on HIGH for 1 minute, whisk several times during cooking, until slightly thickened; do not boil. Serve sauce immediately spooned over fresh fruit.

Makes about 1½ cups.

GOLDEN PECAN SAUCE

Recipe unsuitable to freeze.

1 cup brown sugar, firmly packed
½ cup cream
60g butter
1 tablespoon golden syrup
⅓ cup chopped pecans or walnuts

Combine sugar, cream, butter and golden syrup in a bowl, cook on HIGH for 4 minutes, stir occasionally during cooking; stir in nuts. Serve hot or cold over ice-cream.

Makes about 1½ cups.

SULTANA RUM SAUCE

Recipe unsuitable to freeze.

½ cup castor sugar
½ cup hot water
60g butter
1 teaspoon grated orange rind
¼ cup orange juice
½ cup sultanas
2 tablespoons dark rum

Combine sugar and water in a large bowl, cook on HIGH for 2 minutes; stir to dissolve sugar. Cook on HIGH for about 8 minutes or until syrup turns light golden brown. Stand 5 minutes, add remaining ingredients, stir until butter is melted.

Makes about 1¼ cups.

BERRY ICE-CREAM SAUCE

Sauce can be made up to 3 days ahead. Recipe unsuitable to freeze.

½ cup castor sugar
½ cup hot water
500g fresh or frozen raspberries
1 tablespoon cornflour
1 tablespoon water, extra

Combine sugar and water in a large bowl, cook on HIGH for 5 minutes, stir occasionally. Add berries, cook on HIGH for 4 minutes. Blend cornflour with extra water, add to berry mixture, cook on HIGH for about 2 minutes or until mixture boils and thickens. Serve with ice-cream or cream.

Makes about 3 cups.

LEFT: Clockwise from top: Golden Pecan Sauce; Sultana Rum Sauce; Berry Ice-Cream Sauce. FAR LEFT: Creamy Orange Sauce with Fruit.

ZUCCHINI WALNUT BREAD

Recipe unsuitable to freeze.

90g butter
1¼ cups self-raising flour
1 cup (100g) chopped walnuts
1 cup grated zucchini
¾ cup brown sugar, firmly packed
2 teaspoons grated lemon rind
½ cup buttermilk
1 egg, lightly beaten

Grease a 21cm ring dish. Melt butter in a large bowl on HIGH for 1 minute, stir in sifted flour, walnuts, zucchini, sugar, lemon rind, buttermilk and egg. Spread mixture into prepared dish, cook on MEDIUM HIGH for about 9 minutes or until just set, cover, stand 10 minutes before turning onto wire rack. Serve with butter.

PUMPKIN PECAN MUFFINS

You will need to cook about 300g pumpkin for this recipe; do not add milk or butter when mashing. Recipe unsuitable to freeze.

1½ cups self-raising flour
½ teaspoon ground cinnamon
½ teaspoon mixed spice
⅓ cup brown sugar
⅓ cup oil
2 eggs, lightly beaten
¾ cup mashed pumpkin
½ cup chopped pecans
¼ cup cream
¼ cup chopped pecans, extra

Grease a muffin dish. Sift dry ingredients into large bowl, stir in sugar, then oil, eggs, pumpkin, pecans and cream. Two-thirds fill each muffin container with mixture. Sprinkle with extra pecans. Cook on HIGH for about 3 minutes or until just firm. Stand 1 minute, turn onto wire rack. Repeat with remaining mixture. Serve with butter.

Makes about 12.

Tiles: Northbridge Ceramic & Marble Centre

Left: Zucchini Walnut Bread; right: Pumpkin Pecan Muffins.

CHOC-RUM AND RAISIN ICE-CREAM

Recipe can be made up to a week ahead; keep, covered, in freezer.

⅓ cup chopped raisins
1 tablespoon dark rum
150g dark chocolate, chopped
2 eggs
2 tablespoons castor sugar
300ml carton thickened cream
1 teaspoon vanilla essence
50g dark chocolate, chopped, extra

Combine raisins and rum in a small bowl, cook on HIGH for 1 minute, cool. Melt chocolate on HIGH for 1½ minutes, cool. Whisk eggs and sugar together in a large bowl until thick and creamy, then cook on HIGH for about 1 minute or until slightly thickened, stir occasionally; cool.

Beat cream and essence together until soft peaks form. Fold into egg mixture with raisin mixture, chocolate, and extra chocolate. Pour into a loaf pan, cover with foil, freeze overnight.

Choc-Rum and Raisin Ice-Cream.

Glassware: Incorporated Agencies

GLOSSARY

Some terms, names and alternatives are included here to help everyone use our recipes perfectly.

BACON
Rashers: bacon slices.

BAILEYS ORIGINAL IRISH CREAM: a cream and whisky-based liqueur.

BEEF
Eye fillet: tenderloin.
Mince: ground beef.

BEETROOT: regular round beet.

BICARBONATE OF SODA: baking soda, a component of baking powder.

BREADCRUMBS
Stale: use 1 or 2 day old white or wholemeal bread made into crumbs by grating, blending or processing.
Packaged: use commercially packaged breadcrumbs or cornflake crumbs.

BUCKWHEAT: seeds are roasted and used whole or made into flour; cracked wheat can be substituted.

BUTTER: we used salted butter (sweet) unless otherwise specified; a good quality cooking margarine can be used. 125g butter is equal to 1 stick butter.

BUTTERMILK: the liquid left from the milk from which cream was made. It is now made by adding culture to skim milk to give a slightly acid flavour; skim milk can be substituted, if preferred.

CHEESE
Tasty: use a hard cheddar cheese.
Parmesan: a hard Italian cheese, available grated or by the piece; the piquant flavour is more intense when freshly grated.

CHICKEN: numbers indicate the weight. For example: No. 13 chicken weighs 1.3kg. This applies to all poultry.
Chicken Maryland: a chicken piece consisting of the joined leg and thigh.

CHILLI
Sauce: we used the hot Asian variety except where sweet chilli sauce is used.
Powder: we used the hot Asian variety.
Fresh: use rubber gloves when handling fresh chillies as they can burn your skin. The seeds are the hottest part; remove them if you want to reduce the heat in a recipe. Use half teaspoon chilli powder instead of 1 medium chilli, if preferred.

CHOCOLATE
Choc Bits: small buds of compound dark chocolate.
Dark: we used good cooking chocolate.

CHORIZO SAUSAGES: Spanish and Mexican highly spiced pork sausages seasoned with garlic, cayenne pepper, chilli, etc. They are ready to eat when bought. If unavailable, use a spicy salami.

COCONUT CREAM: available in cans in supermarkets and Asian stores; coconut milk can be substituted although it is not as thick and creamy.

CORNFLOUR: cornstarch.

CREAM: we have specified thickened (whipping) cream when necessary in recipes; cream is simply a light pouring cream, also known as half'n'half.
Sour: a thick commercially cultured soured cream.
Light sour: a less dense commercially cultured soured cream.

CUSTARD POWDER: pudding mix.

EGGPLANT: aubergine.

ESSENCE: extract.

FIVE SPICE POWDER: ground spices which include cinnamon, cloves, fennel, star anise and Szechwan pepper.

FLOUR
Plain flour: all-purpose flour.
Self-raising flour: substitute plain (all-purpose) flour and baking powder in the proportion of three-quarters metric cup plain flour to 2 level metric teaspoons baking powder; sift together several times before using. If using an 8oz measuring cup, use 1 cup plain flour to 2 level metric teaspoons baking powder.

FRESH HERBS: we have specified when to use fresh, dried or ground herbs. We used dried (not ground) herbs in the proportion of 1:4 for fresh herbs, for example, 1 teaspoon dried herbs instead of 4 teaspoons (1 tablespoon) finely chopped fresh herbs.

GINGER, FRESH: ginger root.

GOLDEN SYRUP: maple/pancake syrup or honey can be substituted.

GRAVY POWDER: a flour-based product used to colour and thicken sauces, gravies, etc.

GRILL, GRILLER: broil, broiler.

NUTS
Ground almonds/hazelnuts: we used packaged commercially ground nuts in our recipes unless otherwise specified.

HOISIN SAUCE: a thick sweet Chinese barbecue sauce made from salted black beans, onions and garlic.

KUMARA: a variety of sweet potato, orange in colour.

LAMB
Chump chops: chops cut from the chump section, between the leg and mid-loin.
Cutlets: chops cut from the rib loin.
Fillets: the "eye" from the loin.
Leg chops: cut from top part of the leg.
Loin chops: chops cut from the mid loin below the rib loin.
Noisettes: a loin chop with the bone removed and the "tail" wrapped around the meaty centre part.
Racks: joined cutlets from rib loin.
Shanks: cut from the forelegs.

LEMON BUTTER: lemon curd or cheese.

MIXED SPICE: a finely ground combination of spices which includes allspice, nutmeg and cinnamon; used as an ingredient in sweet recipes.

MUESLI: granola.

MUSTARD
Seeded: a French style of mustard containing crushed mustard seeds.
Dry: a powdered mustard.
Prepared: use mustard of your choice, for example, hot English, French, German.

OIL: we used a light polyunsaturated salad oil in our recipes unless otherwise stated.

PASTRAMI: highly seasoned smoked beef ready to eat when bought.

PEPPERS: capsicums or bell peppers.

PIMENTO: allspice.

PIMIENTOS: canned or bottled peppers.

PORK
Butterfly: skinless, boneless mid-loin chop, split in half and opened out flat.
Fillet: skinless, boneless eye fillet cut from the loin.
Medallions: skinless, boneless, round medallions cut from the loin.
Spareribs: cut from the ribs.
Steaks, schnitzels: usually cut from the leg or rump.

PROSCIUTTO: Uncooked, unsmoked ham cured in salt, ready to eat when bought.

PUMPKIN: we used several varieties; any type can be substituted for the other.

PUNNET: small basket usually holding about 250g fruit.

RICE, BASMATI: a light-textured, delicately flavoured slender grain rice from Pakistan; white long grain rice can be substituted, if desired.

SAMBAL OELEK: a paste made from ground chillies and salt.

SAUCES
Barbecue sauce: we used a commercial sauce, it is usually based on tomato, sugar and vinegar.
Black bean sauce: based on soya sauce and contains black soya beans and salt.
Chilli sauce: we used the hot Asian variety

GLOSSARY

except where sweet chilli sauce is used.
Oyster sauce: a rich brown sauce made from oysters cooked in salt and soya sauce, then thickened with starches.
Plum sauce: a dipping sauce which consists of plums preserved in vinegar, sweetened with sugar and flavoured with chillies and spices.
Satay-style barbecue sauce: is based on soya sauce, peanuts and oil, chilli, garlic and spices.
Soya sauce: is made from fermented soya beans. The light sauce is generally used with white meat dishes and the dark variety with red meat dishes. The dark soya is generally used for colour and the light for flavour.
Tamarind sauce: is made from the acid-tasting fruit of the tamarind tree. If unavailable, soak about 30g dried tamarind in a cup of water, stand 10 minutes. Squeeze the pulp as dry as possible and use the flavoured water.
Teriyaki sauce: is based on the lighter Japanese soya sauce; it also contains sugar, spices and vinegar.
Tomato sauce: tomato ketchup.

SAVOIARDI BISCUITS: also known as Savoy biscuits, lady's fingers or sponge fingers, they are Italian-style crisp fingers made from sponge cake mixture.

SESAME OIL: made from roasted, crushed white sesame seeds, is an aromatic golden-coloured oil with a nutty flavour. It is always used in small quantities. It is not the same as the sesame oil sold in health food stores and should not be used to fry food. It is a flavouring and can be bought in supermarkets and Asian food stores.

SHALLOTS
Golden shallots: a member of the onion family with a delicate onion/garlic flavour.
Green shallots: known as spring onions in some Australian States; scallions in some other countries.

SMALL STOCK CUBE: equivalent to 1 teaspoon powdered bouillon.

SNOW PEAS: also known as mange tout, sugar peas or Chinese peas; are small flat pods with barely formed peas; they are eaten whole. Top, tail and string snow peas. Cook for a short time only.

SPINACH
English spinach: a soft-leafed vegetable, more delicate in taste than silverbeet (spinach); however, young silverbeet can be substituted for English spinach.
Silverbeet: a large-leafed vegetable; remove white stalk before cooking.

SUGAR
Castor: fine granulated table sugar.
Crystal: coarse granulated table sugar.
Icing: confectioners' or powdered sugar. We used icing sugar mixture (not pure) in the recipes in this book.

SULTANAS: seedless white raisins.

SWEET BISCUITS: any plain sweet biscuit (or cookie) can be used.

TOMATO PUREE: known as tomato sauce in some other countries. You can use canned tomato purée or a purée of fresh, ripe tomatoes made by blending or processing the required amount.

TOMATO SUPREME: a canned product consisting of tomatoes, onions, celery, peppers and seasonings.

VEAL
Chops: cut from the rib and loin.
Cutlets: cut from the rib and loin.
Nut of veal: boneless piece cut from leg.
Steaks, schnitzels: cut from the leg.

WHOLEMEAL: wholewheat.

WINE: we used good red and white wines.

WONTON WRAPPERS: thin squares or rounds of fresh noodle dough, yellow in colour. They are sold frozen; cover with a damp cloth to prevent drying while using.

ZUCCHINI: courgette.

CUP AND SPOON MEASURES

Recipes in this book use this standard metric equipment approved by the Australian Standards Association:
(a) 250 millilitre cup for measuring liquids. A litre jug (capacity 4 cups) is also available.
(b) a graduated set of four cups — measuring 1 cup, half, third and quarter cup — for items such as flour, sugar etc. When measuring in these fractional cups, level off at the brim.
(c) a graduated set of four spoons: tablespoon (20 millilitre liquid capacity), teaspoon (5 millilitre), half and quarter teaspoons.

All spoon measurements are level.
Note: We have used large eggs with an average weight of 61g each in all recipes.

OVEN TEMPERATURES

Electric Temperatures	Celsius	Fahrenheit	Gas Temperatures	Celsius	Fahrenheit
Very slow	120	250	Very slow	120	250
Slow	150	300	Slow	150	300
Moderately slow	160-180	325-350	Moderately slow	160	325
Moderate	180-200	375-400	Moderate	180	350
Moderately hot	210-230	425-450	Moderately hot	190	375
Hot	240-250	475-500	Hot	200	400
Very hot	260	525-550	Very hot	230	450

INDEX

INDEX

FRONT COVER: Creamy Ham and Mushroom Pasta, p52; Fresh Buttered Mustard Corn, p54; Corn 'n' Raisin Chicken, p102; Strawberry Mallow Creams, p106.
INSIDE FRONT COVER: Apricot Puddings with Lemon Cream Sauce, p118.
BACK COVER: One-Bowl Chocolate Cake, p112.